Answer Book

How Do They Get Wild Animals for the Circus and the Zoo?

How Can a Fly Walk on the Ceiling?

What Happens Inside a Cat When It Purrs?

Are Sharks Dangerous?

Where Did the Moon Come From?

How Can Ducks Swim Without Having Lessons?

What Happens to Robins in Winter?

What Makes a Firefly's Light?

What Is Atomic Energy?

How Does a Snake Move?

Do Animals Talk to Each Other?

Why Do Beavers Build Dams?

The

Answer Book

By *Mary Elting*

Illustrations by *Tran Mawicke,
John Ballantine, Erwin Hoffman,
William Bryant, Stanley Polczak*

GROSSET & DUNLAP • Publishers • NEW YORK

INTRODUCTION

TO EVERY BOY AND GIRL WHO LIKES TO ASK QUESTIONS

The many interesting things that are all about us bring questions to our minds faster than anybody can answer them for us. Miss Elting knows that boys and girls like to ask questions and she knows what kind of questions you like to ask. To help you find answers to your questions she wrote *The Answer Book*.

If you wonder what makes corn pop and bounce out of your popper, you can find the answer in this book. If you wonder why the cowbird leaves her eggs and her young for other birds to care for, you will find the reason why.

If you have watched a geyser in Yellowstone Park and wondered why its hot water shoots high into the air, you can find, in this book, the explanation you have been wanting.

You will enjoy reading the answers to questions other boys and girls have asked, too. You will learn how the tree frog builds a little swimming pool for her young tadpoles before she lays her eggs. You will discover why waves, strong enough to knock you down, come in at your favorite beach on days when there is no wind to ruffle the water.

And you will find out how rocket engines work and how scientists have discovered how fast a rocket must travel in order to reach the moon.

This exciting world brings many questions to our minds. *The Answer Book* brings us many of the answers.

Emily V. Baker
Curriculum Consultant
Office of the County Superintendent of Schools
San Bernardino, California

1977 Printing

ISBN: 0-448-02864-6 (TRADE EDITION)
ISBN: 0-448-03911-7 (LIBRARY EDITION)

FOREWORD

A QUESTION is a wonderful thing. Where would we be without questions? Suppose nobody had ever said to himself, "I wonder why the birds can fly and I can't." What if nobody had ever wondered about fire — or lightning — or how to say, "I'm hungry"?

A question is one of the most useful things in the world. So is an answer. But no one ever needs to feel ashamed of saying, "I don't know." There are many things that even the greatest scientists have to admit they don't know — yet. The fun of answering really starts when you say, "I'm not sure, but let's see if we can find out."

Some questions can be puzzlers. Listen to a few that boys and girls have asked and see if you can answer them:

What happens to a noise after you can't hear it?

How do they catch air to put in your tires?

How could my brother get chicken pox when he was exposed to the measles?

How high is the sky?

Why doesn't water drip off the bottom of the world?

How could the first bug be born and no one could lay an egg?

How does the world go round and round, and yet my back door is always in the same place?

A book with answers to this special sort of question would be fun, because first you'd have to be a detective and find out what the questioner really wants to know. But *The Answer Book* tries to do something else. It tries to take up the questions that are asked over and over, time and again in families where busy parents can't puzzle out explanations for all the things that young people wonder about. I have tried to make my explanations as clear and accurate as possible. They have been read over by Robert Mueller, scientist and writer, and by Oakes A. White, Curator of Natural History at the Brooklyn Children's Museum. To both of them go my thanks for their help and suggestions. If errors remain in the book, they are my own. If, as I hope, these questions and answers raise more questions, most librarians will be able to supply lists of books for further reading which will entertain young people and educate their elders.

— *Mary Elting*

Contents

CHAPTER I

Traveling Into Space

WHY DO PEOPLE WANT TO GO TO THE MOON?

You know how you feel when someone gives you a present. You can hardly wait to find out what's in the package. That is how scientists feel about the moon, which has a vast number of secrets waiting to be learned.

Why do some of the moon's great mountain ranges run in absolutely straight lines? What caused the deep round holes called craters which spot the moon's face? Why do splashes of lines, like the spokes of a bicycle wheel, spread out from some of the moon's craters? From one particular crater a dark shimmering cloud rises every day, as if millions of insects or birds were swarming up through a hole in the ground. We know that the moon has no life on it, but what is this cloud made of?

These are only a few of the mysteries that can be studied when scientists reach the moon. It's easy to see why they can hardly wait for the day to come.

WHAT IS AN ASTRONAUT?

AN ASTRONAUT is a space man. Only a few astronauts have actually piloted a space craft. Many others are studying about space travel. They talk by radio to a pilot while he is in the space capsule and help to guide him safely back to earth again.

WHAT IS A SATELLITE?

A SATELLITE is an object that travels through space, and it always moves around and around something else that is bigger. The path a satellite follows is called its orbit. The moon travels in an orbit around the earth. It is a satellite of the earth. The earth moves in an orbit around the sun. It is one of the sun's satellites. Most orbits are oval-shaped, not perfect circles.

Men can now create new satellites. When an object shot out into space begins to circle around the sun, the moon, or the earth itself, we say that scientists have "put a satellite into orbit."

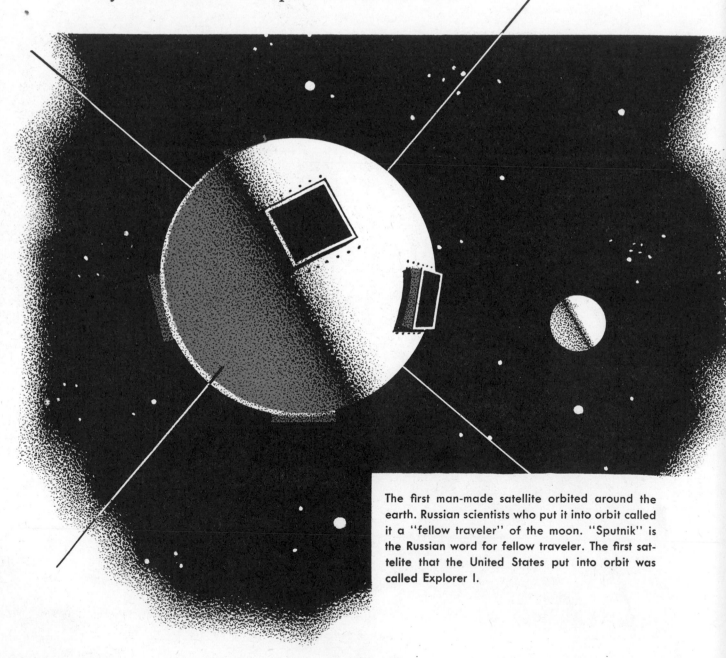

The first man-made satellite orbited around the earth. Russian scientists who put it into orbit called it a "fellow traveler" of the moon. "Sputnik" is the Russian word for fellow traveler. The first satellite that the United States put into orbit was called Explorer I.

WHY DOES A SPACE ROCKET GO SO FAST?

Up, up goes a rocket. Its powerful engines thrust it upward, fighting against the downward pull of earth's gravity. Higher, higher — the pull of gravity grows weaker. The rocket travels faster, faster. At last it is going 25,000 miles an hour. That is nearly seven miles a second. Such a blast of speed kicks the rocket beyond the place where gravity can slow it down enough to make it fall back to earth. The rocket has escaped! Now it can go coasting easily through space.

Does a rocket *have* to go so fast in order to escape gravity? No, it could travel much more slowly, provided it had the right kind of fuel. Some of the old-fashioned fuels are too heavy. A space ship couldn't carry enough of these fuels to keep it traveling slowly until it got beyond the pull of earth's gravity. What about atomic fuel? Atomic fuel is light, but all the ordinary atomic engines would be too heavy. Inventors have had the problem of making a light space-ship engine to go with this wonderful light fuel.

HOW DOES A ROCKET ENGINE WORK?

YOU CAN make a kind of rocket engine. All you need is a toy balloon.

Blow air into the balloon. The more you blow the bigger it gets. That is because air inside it pushes hard against the thin rubber wall and stretches the balloon out, round and fat.

Now stop blowing. Let the balloon go. It will dart away from you with a whoosh. What makes it fly? Look at the pictures and you will see.

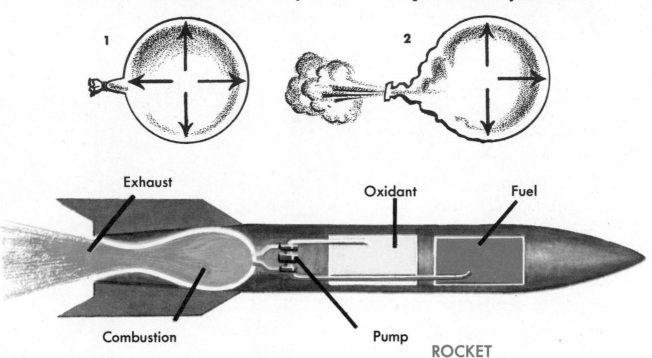

ROCKET

In the first picture the arrows show air pushing against the whole inside wall of the balloon. In the second picture the air at the back of the balloon has nothing to push against. It spurts out through the hole. But air at the front keeps on pushing. It pushes the whole balloon forward.

In a real rocket engine, fiery hot gases are made when the rocket's fuel burns. With a sudden roar the gases spurt out through a hole in the back. And at the same time, the gases are pushing at the front end, too. And this sends the rocket flying up and away.

Scientists have discovered that rockets work according to a rule. The rule says that any push in one direction causes an equal push in the other direction.

14

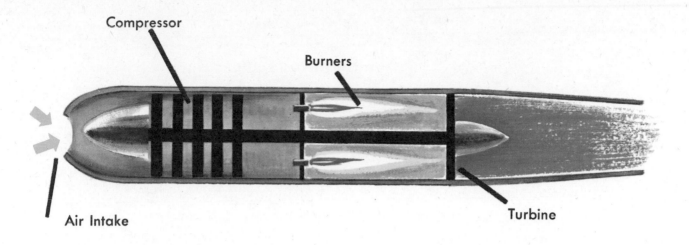

Compressor

Burners

Air Intake

Turbine

JET ENGINE

IS A JET ENGINE THE SAME AS A ROCKET?

LOOK AT the picture of a rocket and you will see how it gets its push forward. Fuel burning inside it makes the push. A jet engine gets its push in the same way. However, there is a difference between jets and rockets. A jet engine needs oxygen to burn its fuel, and it gets the oxygen from the air *outside*. A rocket carries *inside* itself everything it needs to make its fuel burn.

Now you can see why space ships must have rocket engines. A rocket can go far out into space where there is no air. It can keep running on its own supplies.

15

CAN PEOPLE BUILD CITIES ON THE MOON?

SOME DAY PEOPLE will certainly try to build settlements on the moon. A good place for houses in a moon town will be a cave or a tunnel. Underground houses will not be squashed by meteorites that constantly fall on the moon from outer space. The temperature in a cave doesn't change as much as the temperature outside. This will be important on the moon, since daytime there is so hot that food could be cooked on the rocks, and the nights get bitterly cold.

Pioneer moon homes may be made of airtight plastic that can be blown up like a balloon inside the cave. The reason for this is that the moon has no air around it. The pioneers will have to take along from earth the oxygen they need for breathing. They will wear oxygen masks when they are away from home. But the balloon house itself will be filled with air. Perhaps the house will have beds, tables and chairs built into it. These can be inflated, too. Scientists hope they can make oxygen from the moon's rocks, after they get settled there.

Moon-house building will be easy. The moon's gravity is less than earth's gravity. And so everything weighs only one-sixth as much.

ARE ASTEROIDS THE SAME AS PLANETS?

AN ASTEROID *is* a planet — a very small one. Asteroids travel around the sun in regular orbits, just as the earth and the other full-sized planets do. There are thousands and thousands of these small planets. A few of them have been given lovely names. For example, Vesta, Juno, Gaussia, Piazzia. Scientists believe that asteroids are really the broken, lumpy pieces of one big planet which somehow got smashed ages ago.

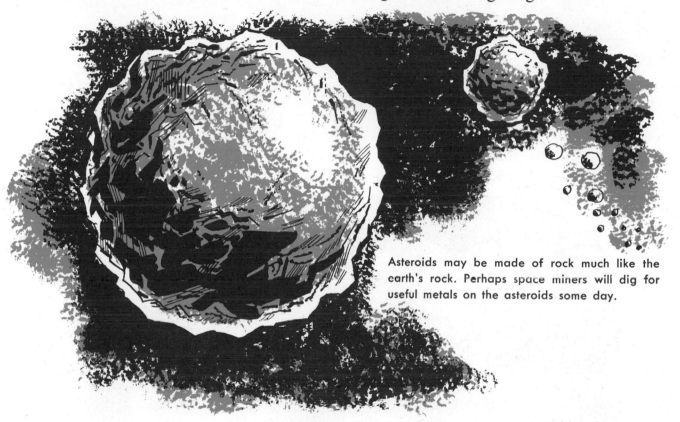

Asteroids may be made of rock much like the earth's rock. Perhaps space miners will dig for useful metals on the asteroids some day.

CAN SPACE TRAVELERS LIVE ON PILLS INSTEAD OF FOOD?

JUST AS an experiment, men have tried living on pills for a while. The pills contained dried, condensed foods — everything necessary to keep the body healthy. Scientists thought the pills might be just the thing for space travelers. But the experiment didn't last long. The men found a pill diet so unsatisfying that they began to feel cross and quarrelsome. Perhaps astronauts *could* live on pills, but they won't unless they have to.

IS IT SAFE TO LIVE IN A SPACE SHIP WITHOUT GRAVITY?

IF YOU WERE traveling in a space capsule around the earth, you would feel as if you didn't weigh anything at all. Your weight on earth comes from the pull of gravity. But a special thing happens when the capsule goes around and around in orbit. The effect of gravity on you disappears. And so you are weightless. You get somewhat the feeling of being weightless when you come down from the top of a tall building in a very fast elevator.

Astronauts who have been weightless say that it is quite pleasant, once they are used to it. But doctors don't know for sure whether it is healthy to be without the pull of gravity for months at a time. Perhaps when astronauts begin making long journeys through space, their ships will carry machinery to make the men feel as if gravity is pulling on them.

A weightless astronaut behaves like this unless he is strapped to his seat. The slightest push will send him up, down, sideways.

HOW LONG WOULD IT TAKE TO GO TO MARS IN A SPACE SHIP?

How LONG does it take to go from your house to the store? It depends on how fast you go, of course. Suppose a space ship travels a thousand miles an hour. At that rate the journey to Mars would take about six years.

But a rocket can go much faster than that. The first one to reach outer space traveled 25,000 miles an hour. A rocket ship going at that speed could take you to Mars in about three months.

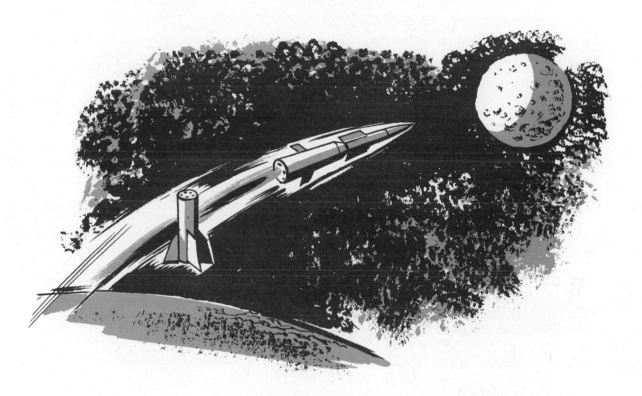

CAN PEOPLE EVER VISIT OTHER SOLAR SYSTEMS?

SOME SCIENTISTS say, "Of course not!" A journey to the neighborhood of the nearest star would take more than 100,000 years in a space ship that traveled 25,000 miles an hour.

But space ships may some day go much faster than that. One scientist believes it is possible to build an engine that will drive a ship two million miles an hour! But even at that speed the trip to the nearest star would take more than 125 years.

WHAT GOOD ARE SPACE SHIPS?

SPACE SHIPS may do many very useful things. They may serve as power plants, capturing energy from the sun and passing it along to be used here on earth. Weathermen in space ships may find out a great deal about the weather on earth. They may even find ways of changing it. Scientists may make important discoveries about metals by studying how the extreme cold of space affects them.

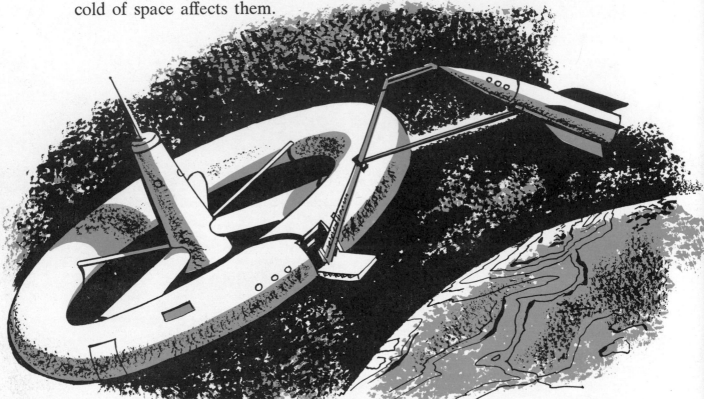

We can make a long list of useful things that men found after they discovered North and South America. Columbus couldn't think up nearly so long a list of the things he *hoped* to discover when he set out from Spain to cross the Atlantic. He couldn't even say he intended to look for America because he didn't know there was such a place. It may be the same with space explorers and their ships. They may make discoveries they couldn't dream were possible before they left the earth.

Satellites have already sent back messages that have astonished the scientists. They used to think that the earth was shaped like an orange, flattened on top and bottom. But measurements made by the satellites tell us that the earth is shaped like a pear instead.

ARE OTHER PLANETS LIKE THE EARTH?

WHEN THE FIRST explorers visit another planet they will certainly find it different from the earth. We don't know exactly what visitors might see on any of the planets, but here are some of the scientists' guesses.

Thick heavy clouds surround Venus. The planet's surface may be one great desert. Or it may be a landless ocean — or a vast jungle of strange plants that grow in spite of poison gases in the atmosphere.

Jupiter and Saturn also have cloudy atmospheres. They are very cold. Neptune, Uranus and Pluto are even colder. They may be like gigantic snowballs made of ice and frozen gases with centers of hard rock. Mercury on the other hand, is very hot. It is made of rock and is probably something like the moon.

A visitor to Mars might feel more at home. Mars probably has growing plants which change color with the seasons. Ice caps cover the north and south poles. Do animals live on Mars? Perhaps a camera in a space ship may tell us before visitors land to see for themselves.

Sun

Mercury

Venus

Earth

Mars

Jupiter

Saturn

Uranus

Neptune

Pluto

Gravity on Mars is less than on earth. It would be easy to take twenty-foot strides on Mars. But Jupiter's gravity would slow you down to a creep. There you would feel as if you weighed three times as much as you do on earth.

21

WHAT IS A SHOOTING STAR?

A FLASH of moving light suddenly appears in the sky at night. Then just as suddenly it goes out. In the old days people called it a shooting star, which was a pretty name, but not very accurate. A real star is a great glowing ball of gases thousands of miles thick. A shooting star usually weighs anywhere from a few ounces to a few pounds, and it is made of rock or metal. Scientists call it a meteor.

Thousands of meteors swarm through space, near the earth, day and night. Some of them come so close that the earth's gravity captures them and they begin to fall toward us. But the air acts as a brake and slows them down. The braked meteors get hotter, hotter — till they change to gas in a burst of glowing light. Meteors enter our atmosphere in daytime, too. Their light is too dim to be noticed in the sunlit sky. We know they are there because radar screens locate them.

IS A METEORITE THE SAME AS A SHOOTING STAR?

NOT EXACTLY. A shooting star is usually a small chunk of solid stuff that zooms toward earth out of space and burns up before it reaches the ground. Scientists call it a meteor. But once in a while a really big chunk comes along. It may explode high in the air, and small pieces of it come raining down. These are called meteorites. A few supercolossal meteorites have hit the earth. One of them struck the Arizona desert many hundreds of years ago. It left a hole nearly three-quarters of a mile wide. Another huge one fell in Canada in bygone times. Most meteorites drop into the seas, because there is much more water than land on earth.

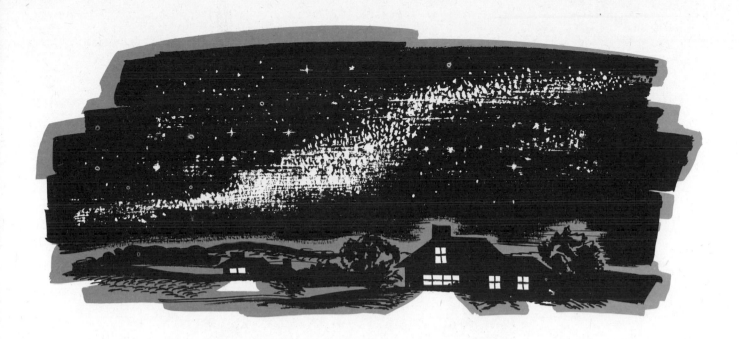

WHAT IS THE MILKY WAY?

ON A CLEAR NIGHT you can see a wide silvery band like a cloud across the sky. This is the Milky Way, and it is made entirely of stars — one hundred billion stars! When we look at the sky we see only part of the Milky Way. If we could see all of it at once, it would appear to be a great wheel, thick at the center and thinning out at the rim. The wheel is called a galaxy. Like everything in space, the galaxy wheel turns constantly. Now let's see where we fit into this picture.

Imagine that the galaxy is a merry-go-round, turning and turning. Near the outside edge of the merry-go-round platform, imagine a spinning top. This top would be the sun. Imagine next that a bee is zooming round and round the spinning top. The bee would be the earth. Finally, imagine that a fruit fly is whizzing round and round the bee. The fruit fly would be the moon circling the earth. Now you have the picture: The moon goes around the earth. Both go around the sun. All three wheel around the hub of the galaxy.

How long does it take for the galaxy to make one complete turn? Two hundred million years!

Perhaps you think there would hardly be room in space for more than one galaxy. Well, take a deep breath. Astronomers think there are a billion galaxies in space, and every galaxy has billions of stars in it.

WHY DON'T THE PLANETS BUMP INTO EACH OTHER?

THE EARTH and all the other planets travel around the sun. Some travel faster than the earth. Some travel more slowly. Each one has its own path — its own orbit. The earth's orbit is just right for its size and speed. So are the orbits of the other planets. The sun and its family of planets all move along as regularly as clockwork. Perhaps there were traffic problems long, long ago when the orbiting first started. Some scientists believe that collisions did happen. But everything moves smoothly now. You need not worry about bumping into Mars.

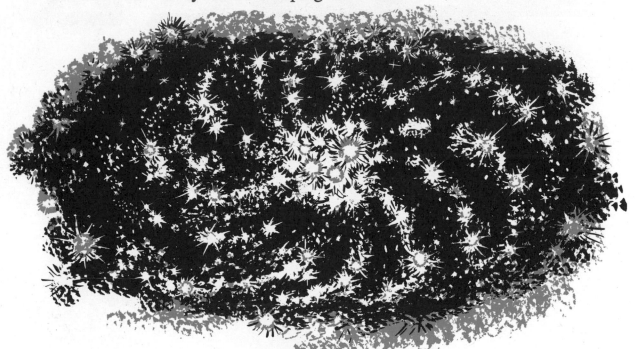

WHAT IS THE UNIVERSE?

THE EARTH and the moon, the other planets, the sun and all the stars together are called the universe. Some of the stars in the universe are so far away that you have to look for them with a telescope. Others are still farther away. You can't see them even with the help of the most powerful telescopes. Then how do we know they are there? Using these same telescopes, and sensitive photographic film, scientists have managed to take pictures of them. Scientists think that very, very far away there may be still more stars waiting to be discovered.

CHAPTER II

The Wonderful Animal World

ARE BATS REALLY BLIND?

"BLIND AS A BAT" is an old-fashioned expression. Bats can really see. But they don't depend on eyesight to guide them when they fly around at night. They depend on the echoes of their own voices.

A bat broadcasts its voice in short, quick squeaks. The squeaks bounce back from any object nearby — even from a telephone wire only a few inches away. The bat's keen ears pick up the echo. Instantly it knows just where the wire is. So it can swerve to one side.

Bats have to hunt for their food in the dark. Some of them eat the nectar of flowers. Others eat moths, mosquitoes or other insects that fly at night. A bat uses echoes to locate the insects.

A bat's voice is too high for our ears to hear, but scientists have used sensitive machines to pick up the sound. They have also done experiments to prove that echo-location works. First they blindfolded a bat. It flew without bumping into anything. Then they taped its ears shut. It flew into obstacles it had missed before.

Some bats have ordinary mouselike faces. Others have complicated queer-looking noses. They probably use these "nose-leaves" to aim their voices.

WHY DO BEAVERS BUILD DAMS?

BEAVERS build dams so that they will have safe homes close to a supply of food in winter. In the pond that forms behind their dam, the father and mother beaver put together a hut. It looks like a jumble of sticks and mud, but it is quite strong. It has a good dry room inside and the entrance is hidden under water. A beaver family — the father, mother and several young ones called kits — live together in the house.

Even in winter when the woods are deep in snow and the pond is frozen over, beavers usually have plenty of food. They eat the bark from tree branches and bushes which they have cut and then anchored in the mud at the bottom of the pond.

A spider has little tubes called spinnerets on its underside. From these spinnerets comes the liquid which hardens in the air to form silk for a web.

WHY DOESN'T A SPIDER GET STUCK IN ITS OWN WEB?

A SPIDER spins two different kinds of silky thread out of its own body, and it uses both kinds when it makes a web. One kind of silk is sticky. Flies, moths and other insects get caught in it. The other kind of silk isn't sticky. The spider walks on threads of the non-sticky silk when it runs across its web. But just in case the spider slips or makes a mistake, it has an oily stuff on its body that keeps it from getting tangled.

Fluke

Striped Bass

This fish moves its strong tail from side to side.

This fish swims by swishing its tail up and down.

HOW DOES A FISH SWIM?

A FISH SWIMS by using the muscles of its powerful tail. The tail fin swishes from side to side. As it moves sideways, the tail also gives a backward push on the water. By pushing back against the water with its tail fin the fish moves itself forward.

Doesn't a fish ever paddle itself along with its other fins? Hardly ever. Most fish use the other fins for steering or balancing. Some use them as feelers when they hunt for food at night.

A fish called the shark-sucker has a fin like a suction cup. The fish sticks its cup onto a shark's body and hitchhikes along until the shark finds something to eat. Any morsels that fall from the shark's mouth are gobbled by the sucker.

The fins of a flying fish act like glider wings when it leaps out of the water and soars through the air.

HOW CAN FROGS STAY UNDER WATER SO LONG?

WHEN A FROG is sitting on the bank of a stream, he breathes through his nostrils as you do. Air goes into his lungs, which are somewhat like your lungs. Then he dives under water, and he doesn't come to the surface as quickly as you have to when you dive. Why not? There is always some air mixed with water in a stream or pond, and a frog can take a little of it into his body through his skin.

Do THIS: Stretch a rubber band between the thumb and a finger of one hand. Then pluck the two strands gently. They wiggle back and forth very fast. (*Vibrate* is the correct word for the wiggling.) When the strands vibrate they make the air vibrate, too, and so you hear a sort of purring noise.

Your cat has little stretchable bands in its throat. These aren't made of rubber, of course. They are a special living part of the cat's body. When a cat feels relaxed and satisfied, it can make the bands vibrate in its throat. As the cat breathes, the air picks up the vibrations, and so the sound of purring is carried through the air to your ears.

Lions and tigers are called big cats. A big cat has an extra set of bones and bands in its throat, just at the back of the tongue. When these vibrate they make a fierce roar.

DO ANIMALS LIVE AS LONG AS PEOPLE?

MOST ANIMALS have very short lives. But some live longer than people usually live. A tortoise has been known to reach the age of one hundred and fifty. Elephants grow old at just about the same rate as people. Many of them live to be sixty-five or seventy. Dogs and cats are old when they reach the age of ten, but some live longer. And one kind of insect — the seventeen-year locust — usually spends seventeen years in the earth before it comes out. Then it lives for only a few weeks.

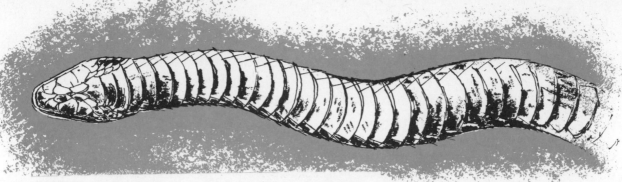

HOW DOES A SNAKE MOVE?

ONE KIND of snake has hard squarish plates on its underside. It uses these instead of feet. Each plate can move a little. The snake lifts a plate, then pushes back with it against the earth. The backward push of the plates shoves the snake forward — the way ski poles shove a skier. Most snakes slither forward by pushing with their many ribs against rough places in the earth.

WHAT MAKES A FIREFLY'S LIGHT?

A FIREFLY'S LIGHT comes from two juices that it makes in its body. Neither kind of juice will shine all by itself, but when the two mix together with air, they glow. A firefly doesn't burn your hand if you catch it. The light is cool, like the light from a fluorescent bulb.

Scientists believe that fireflies attract their mates by flashing their lights. But no one can yet explain a strange habit of fireflies in Thailand. Large numbers of them gather in trees. Then suddenly they all light up at the same moment. On and off, on and off — sometimes several trees full of fireflies will flash in unison.

Another glowing creature is the *ferrocarril* worm that lives in South America. It has eleven pairs of little green lights along its sides and one red light on its head. If you annoy the worm it turns its lights on.

PROBABLY you have heard the story of the fox who had thousands of fleas in his fur. The fleas bit him, and he scratched himself till he grew weary. At last he went to the river bank, picked up a good-sized stick, and holding the stick in his mouth, walked into the water. The fleas all crawled up onto his back to keep dry. The fox went on into deeper water, and the fleas crowded onto his head. He ducked lower and lower, forcing the fleas to scramble down along his nose and finally out onto the stick he held in his teeth. Suddenly, the fox opened his jaws. Away went the stick with his tormentors aboard, and now he had a rest from scratching until a new crop of the pests made their home in his fur.

This sounds like a fairy tale, but naturalists say that some foxes have really learned to get rid of fleas in exactly this way.

DO FISH HAVE VOICES?

FISH CALLED CROAKERS make hoarse "garrumph" sounds. The noise is caused by two muscles that beat on an air-filled sac like a drum in the fish's belly. The drumming can be heard through an instrument called a hydrophone, a sort of underwater microphone. Sometimes the fish keeps on croaking after it is caught and landed.

Scientists recognize the noises made by several kinds of fish. But they are puzzled by certain strange groans and wails that the hydrophone often picks up. They don't yet know what water animal makes these weird sounds.

DOES A CAMEL STORE WATER IN ITS HUMP?

CAMELS can live in the desert for two or three weeks, eating dry food and drinking no water. At the end of that time, a thirsty camel will guzzle enough to fill a bathtub. People used to think that the camel's hump was a sort of natural canteen where the water was stored. But scientists have found that the hump contains fat, not water. A camel lives on this fat when it can't find food in the desert.

Then how can a camel go so long without drinking? The answer is that a camel stores water all over its body — in the flesh and blood and skin and muscles. As it uses the water, its body gets drier and drier. If other animals dry out like this, they get sick. But it doesn't bother the camel at all. In fact, a camel never takes little drinks. It always waits until it is so dry it needs about a bathtub full of water.

A camel's stomach is lined with spongelike cells which hold as much as two gallons of extra water.

Bactrian Camel

The two-humped camel lives in northern Asia. The camel with one hump lives in southern Asia and North Africa. A one-humped racing camel is called a dromedary.

HOW CAN A FLY WALK ON THE CEILING?

A FLY has a little suction cup on each of its six feet. This is how the suction cup works: It is hollow inside and slightly moist. When it is pushed against a flat surface, most of the air is squeezed out. The moisture seals the edges and keeps air from getting back in. Now there is a lot of air outside and very little inside the cup. The pressure of the outside air is strong. It holds the suction cup tightly to the ceiling.

The fly picks up three of its feet at a time to step forward. The suction cups on the other three feet hold the fly in place till their turn to move. Does this seem like a hard way to walk? It would be hard for us, but not for a fly. Flies have great strength for their size.

WHY IS A SNAKE ALWAYS STICKING ITS TONGUE OUT?

A SNAKE'S TONGUE is a kind of special feeler. It helps to detect smells. The tongue darts out of the mouth and picks up bits of dust. Then it draws in and places the dust on certain spots in the mouth. These spots are very sensitive to odors. So the tongue gives the snake an extra keen sense of smell.

The forked red tongue looks dangerous, but it can't do you any harm, even though it belongs to a rattlesnake. A poisonous snake can harm you only if it bites you with its sharp hollow fangs.

Spider Monkey

Gray Squirrel

Fat-tailed Sheep

WHAT ARE TAILS FOR?

DIFFERENT ANIMALS use their tails in very different ways. A spider monkey can swing from its tail as if it were an extra hand or foot. A common opossum can do the same, and there is one kind of opossum in South America which uses tails as a way to keep a family together. Baby opossums wrap their little tails around their mother's big tail, and they hang on no matter where she drags them.

Cats and squirrels seem to use their tails to help them balance when they jump. A fish swims with its tail, of course, and so do other water creatures. A horse switches his tail to keep flies away, and you often see two horses standing side by side, shooing flies off each other. A beaver slaps its broad flat tail on the water to warn other beavers of danger.

One kind of sheep has a very different use for its tail which happens to be very fat. It serves as a storehouse of food. The sheep's body can live on the fat for quite a while if the supply of grass runs out.

A peacock seems to have its beautiful tail for pure decoration.

DO ANIMALS TALK TO EACH OTHER?

PEOPLE ARE the only animals that talk in words and sentences. But many animals do give signals to each other. For example, a starling screams when it is frightened. The cry of alarm warns other starlings of danger. A mother cat makes a special kind of meow when she calls her kittens. Horses whinny to greet their companions. Crickets attract their mates with a noise they make by rubbing the sawtoothed edge of one wing across the ridges in the opposite wing. Many birds sing to attract mates.

Bees have a kind of silent "sign language." A professor in Germany discovered it. He noticed that sometimes a bee would come to the hive and perform an excited little dance. The other bees would pay close attention. Then they would fly off straight to a field full of flowers that the first bee had located. The professor studied the dances. Right turns, left turns, little jumps — all had a meaning. The dancing bee was giving directions to a place where nectar could be gathered from flowers. In the end, the professor understood the sign language so well that he himself could go to the field the bee had discovered!

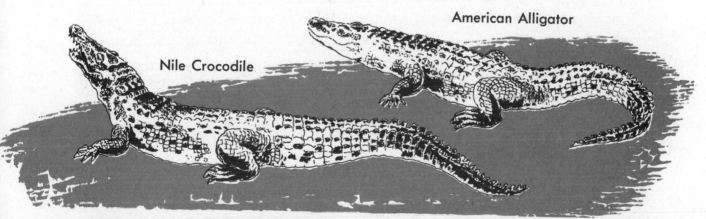

American Alligator

Nile Crocodile

ARE ALLIGATORS THE SAME AS CROCODILES?

THE TWO CREATURES are alike in some ways, and they are related, but they also have important differences. An easy way to tell them apart is this: A crocodile — but not an alligator — has notches in its upper jaw. These let teeth in the lower jaw show, even when the mouth is shut. A crocodile has a longer, sharper snout than an alligator.

WHY DO COWBIRDS LAY EGGS IN THE NESTS OF OTHER BIRDS?

MOST MOTHER BIRDS sit on their eggs to keep them warm so they will hatch, but a mother cowbird never does this. She doesn't even build a nest of her own. Instead she lays one egg in each of four or five different birds' nests. Then she flies off and never comes back. Other birds always egg-sit and baby-sit for her. This is strange, but there is a reason for it.

Before people killed off the buffalo that used to roam on the plains by the million, the cowbird was really the buffalo bird. Its main food was a little wormlike creature that lived under the skin of the buffalo. To get this food the bird naturally had to be where the buffalo were, and the buffalo always kept moving in search of grass.

The mother buffalo bird could not eat her usual food and raise a family at the same time. But by leaving her eggs in the care of a foster mother the buffalo bird gained freedom to look for food, and her babies grew up all right.

When the buffalo disappeared, the birds had a problem. They had to find a new kind of food. This they managed to do, and instead of following buffalo they followed cows. That, of course, is where the name comes from. But cowbirds didn't change their old egg-laying habits.

The buffalo had itchy skins, and telegraph poles made wonderful scratching posts. The only trouble was that buffalo were such big animals they pushed the poles over. In the old days many a telegram was late because some cowbird had not found a little worm under the skin of some big buffalo.

HOW CAN GRASSHOPPERS MAKE SO MUCH NOISE?

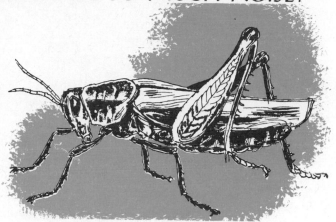

FOR A SMALL CREATURE a grasshopper makes a big racket. He simply rubs his hind legs across his wings. Each leg has a rough edge, somewhat like the teeth of a comb. Each wing has ridges like the ridges on corrugated cardboard. Try scratching a comb across a piece of cardboard. You'll see just how a grasshopper makes his rasping sound. Only males are noisy. A female grasshopper merely listens — with ears that are not on each side of her head, but on each side of her body.

WHEN A TURTLE SLEEPS IN THE MUD ALL WINTER, HOW CAN IT BREATHE?

THE ANSWER IS—it does *not* breathe. The kind of turtle that spends the winter in the mud actually does hold its breath. When cold weather comes, the turtle burrows into swampy earth and goes to sleep. The beating of its heart slows down till it almost stops. Its whole body keeps so still that it can get along without any fresh air until it wakes up and crawls out of the mud in spring.

Sleeping all winter is called hibernation. Woodchucks and some other animals hibernate in their holes. Their bodies slow down, but they keep on breathing. Bears take short naps, but they don't really hibernate.

A lungfish also burrows into the mud and goes to sleep, but not in winter. It sleeps in summer. The lungfish can take oxygen from the air instead of from water. When its pond dries up it can stay alive in its burrow. Unlike the box turtle, it breathes when it sleeps.

WHAT HAPPENS TO ROBINS IN WINTER?

IF YOU LIVE in a place where winter is cold, you know that robins disappear before the snow falls. They fly away south to warmer country where they can find plenty of worms and insects to eat. In spring the robins come back. This moving back and forth is called migration.

Many kinds of birds migrate in huge flocks. Each kind follows just about the same path each year. Some travel only a few hundred miles. Others fly immense distances. Often a bird will find its way back to its old nesting place year after year.

How can we be so sure the same bird comes back? We can be sure if the bird wears a label. Naturalists actually do put labels on birds. They fasten tiny aluminum bands to the birds' legs. Each band has a different number. Every year naturalists catch birds and look at the bands. They can tell by the number whether a particular bird has come back to its old home.

Why don't the birds get lost? One kind of bird guides itself by the stars. The positions of the stars give it directions, just as the Pole Star tells us which way is north. Scientists still have to find out whether all birds are guided in this same way.

The arctic tern is the champion migrator. It builds its nest in the far north — in the arctic. Then it flies south for 11,000 miles to the antarctic. Next year it covers those same 11,000 miles to the arctic again.

The golden plover migrates from Canada to South America in autumn. It flies 2,000 miles in two days and two nights, and it doesn't stop to rest or eat along the way!

CHAPTER III

How Does It Work?

THE THERMOMETER on your wall is a glass tube with a silvery or red or blue line inside. The silvery line is a liquid called mercury. Since the tube is hollow, the mercury can move. It goes up as the room gets warm and down when the room turns cold. A thermometer with a colored line contains a different liquid that behaves in the same way.

The marks and numbers on the tube measure the height of the mercury. If it shrinks down to the 32-mark, you will be shivering, and water will turn to ice. But when the mercury goes up as high as 90, you feel very hot.

Why does the line of mercury grow taller or shorter? Like everything else, mercury is made of tiny particles called molecules. The mercury molecules are always moving, bumping into each other and bouncing away. Even when the silvery line remains steady inside the tube, the molecules are shifting around and around. Heat makes them move faster. The fast-bouncing molecules shove each other farther and farther apart. So the mercury takes up more space, and it rises in the tube.

When the molecules get cold they move more slowly. Now they don't need so much bouncing space. They draw closer together, and the mercury goes down.

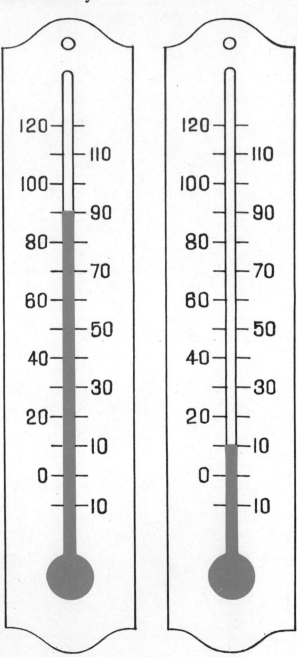

THE BULB in a flashlight looks like a tiny electric light bulb. That's exactly what it is. Perhaps this seems strange. A flashlight doesn't have a wire attached to it, so it can't get electricity from the power plant. But the batteries in a flashlight *are* a kind of power plant. They send electricity through the bulb and make it glow whenever you push the button that turns it on.

How do batteries make electricity? First we have to remember that there are small particles of electricity in everything. These particles, called electrons, can be made to move from one place to another. Electrons streaming through a light bulb light it up.

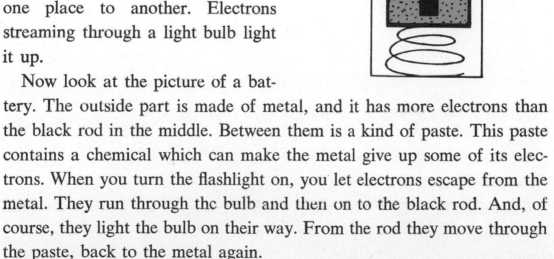

Paste

Metal

Now look at the picture of a battery. The outside part is made of metal, and it has more electrons than the black rod in the middle. Between them is a kind of paste. This paste contains a chemical which can make the metal give up some of its electrons. When you turn the flashlight on, you let electrons escape from the metal. They run through the bulb and then on to the black rod. And, of course, they light the bulb on their way. From the rod they move through the paste, back to the metal again.

The chemical paste is something like a one-way street with a traffic cop who keeps the electrons moving from metal to bulb to rod and back to metal again.

After a battery has been used for a while the chemicals in the paste change. The movement of electrons stops, and we say the battery is dead.

A STRANGE thing happens when you pour hot water onto gelatin powder to make dessert. The powder disappears. You can't see it any more, but it is there. The hot water breaks the powder up into tiny bits, like small strings, so small that you can't see them floating in the water. They are little but strong. As each tiny string gets cool, it acts as if it were a magnet. You have seen a magnet pick up a tack. The invisible strings of gelatin can't pick up tacks, but they *can* pick up water. A bit of water sticks to each string.

If you keep the gelatin cool, it holds the water very tight. But as soon as you heat gelatin, water escapes. When you put the mixture back in the refrigerator, the tiny strings pick up their water drops again.

HOW DOES A NEON SIGN WORK?

A NEON light is something like a fluorescent light. Neon signs are made of glass tubes shaped into words and decorations. When you push a button, the words light up — red, blue, green. The light seems to swirl around inside the tubes. But where does it come from? There is no wire running through the tube as there is in regular electric light bulbs.

The light comes from a gas with which the tube is filled. When electricity goes through this gas, it glows very brightly. A gas called neon gives off a reddish glow, and that is where the name neon light came from. Other gases make lights that are blue or yellow. Yellow light in a blue glass tube looks green. The movement that you see in the tube comes from the gas swirling around.

It takes very little electricity to make the neon tubes light up, and that is why they are used for huge signs.

WHAT MAKES A BALL BOUNCE?

A RUBBER BALL bounces because it is elastic. An elastic substance is made of molecules that do two opposite things: They give when they are pushed, but they also resist being pushed. When a ball hits the floor, the blow flattens it a little. But rubber molecules resist. They push back against the floor. And up goes the ball into the air again, as round as before. You are made of elastic material, too. Think what you would look like if the molecules in your body didn't resist when they are pushed around!

WHAT MAKES POPCORN POP?

STEAM MAKES popcorn pop. That seems like a queer thing to say. Everybody knows popcorn isn't wet. So where does the steam come from? It comes from *inside* each grain of corn.

Before you put a grain of corn in a popper it feels very dry. But there are tiny drops of water inside it. Each drop is so small that you can't see it. Each one is wrapped in a little white jacket that holds it tight.

When a grain of corn gets hot in the popper, the drops of water get hot, too. Soon the water turns to steam. Then pop! The steam bursts out and flies away into the air, leaving a fluffy pile of little white jackets behind.

The American Indians discovered popcorn. Here are some other foods the Indians gave us: Tomatoes, chocolate, squash, pumpkin, pears, potatoes and beans.

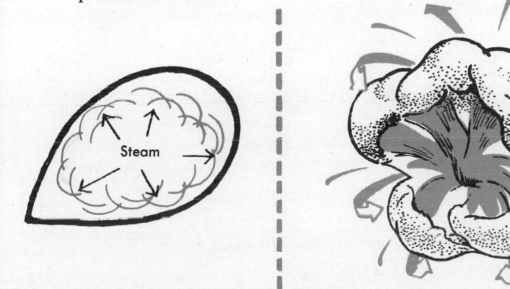

Steam

HOW DOES A LIGHT BULB WORK?

THE WIRE that brings electricity to a light bulb is about as thick as the lead in a pencil. Electric current flows along it with no trouble. Inside a light bulb is a very thin wire. When the current starts to flow through this thin wire, a kind of traffic jam starts. The current pushes and shoves. The harder it shoves, the hotter the thin wire gets. It gets white-hot and begins to glow. The glowing white-hot wire gives us light.

The thin wire grows so hot that it would burn up if it were out in the open air. The glass bulb protects it because all the air has been pumped out of the bulb and a special non-burning gas has been pumped in.

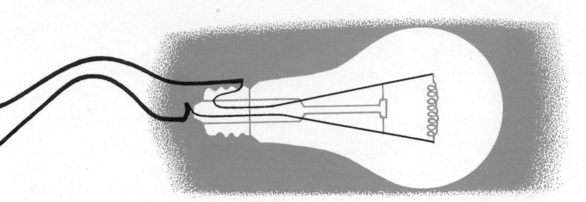

A toaster works something like a light bulb. It, too, has a special kind of wire inside. Instead of getting white-hot when electric current pushes and shoves through it, this wire only gets red-hot, and it doesn't burn up in the open air. If it did, you would have to get a new toaster with every loaf of bread. Electric irons and heaters work in much the same way as toasters.

HOW DO FLUORESCENT LIGHTS WORK?

A FLUORESCENT lamp has a long, thin bulb called a tube. It gives us light with almost no heat.

The tube is filled with a special kind of gas. When electricity goes through this gas, it gives off a dim blue light. Now the blue light strikes the inside surface of the tube which has been covered with a special paint. And a wonderful thing happens. The paint begins to glow! It's not the gas in the fluorescent tube that gives us light; it's not a hot electric wire. It's the paint that shines with a cool, bright light.

WHY DOES A CAT'S FUR SPARKLE WHEN YOU RUB IT IN THE DARK?

THE SPARKLE is a tiny bit of electric light. Everything has two kinds of electricity in it. One kind is called positive, and the other kind is called negative. These two kinds of electricity pull toward each other. But they can often be separated by rubbing two different things together. Your hand rubs the cat's fur. A lot of rubbing can make a lot of negative electricity pile up on your fingers, leaving the positive electricity on the fur. The two kinds of electricity still keep pulling and tugging toward each other. At last the tug is strong enough to make them leap back together in a sudden spark of electric light. Usually the spark is so small you can see it only if the room is dark.

HOW DOES A SWITCH TURN ON THE ELECTRIC LIGHT?

ELECTRICITY comes to your house through a thick wire. Then it runs through a small wire to the bulb in your lamp. The wire is a path for electricity to follow. If nothing stops electricity, it can keep on running into the lamp bulb to make a light. But you don't need a light all the time. So you have a switch that stops electricity when you want to stop it.

A switch is really a little bridge on the path, like a board across a ditch. When you walk down a real path and come to a ditch, you can walk across a board and keep right on going. But suppose somebody snatches the board away. Then you have to stop.

It is the same way with the little metal bridge in the switch. When the bridge is in place, electricity can run over it. But when you snap the switch, you pull the bridge back. You leave a space, like a ditch, and the electricity has to stop until you push the bridge across the space again.

Did you say to yourself a minute ago, "A ditch wouldn't stop me. I'd jump across"? You *can* jump across little ditches, but not across big ones. Electricity can jump across little spaces, too. So the space in the switch is made wide enough to keep the electricity from getting across.

45

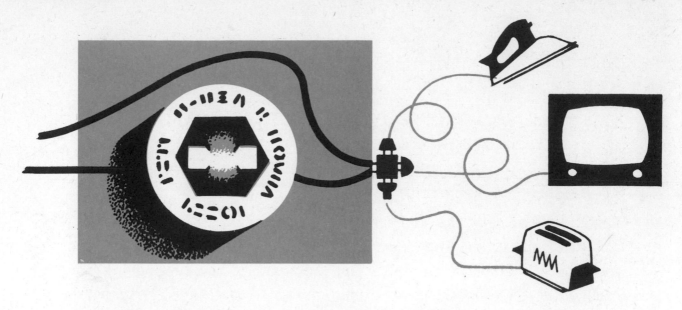

WHAT MAKES A FUSE BURN OUT?

Perhaps this has happened at your house: An electric iron or a toaster or a fan gets something wrong with it — and the lights suddenly go off, too. A fuse has burned out!

A fuse often seems like a nuisance, but it is really a help. Whenever something goes wrong with electricity, the wires in your house are likely to get too hot, and that may start a fire. The fuse is a guard that turns the electricity off if there is danger of fire.

If you look inside a burned fuse, you will see a little broken piece of metal. Before it was broken, electricity from the power line could run through that metal strip on its way into your house. When just the right amount of electricity ran through it, there was nothing to worry about.

Then something happened and too much electricity began to go through the strip. It got too hot, and the metal burned in two. From then on electricity couldn't run through the fuse into the house. So your lights went out.

If you use too many electrical things at once, you make extra electricity run through the wire. A machine that isn't working right, or a broken cord can also make too much electricity surge through the fuse and burn it out.

Suppose the fuse wasn't there. The extra electricity would make the regular wires in your house get very hot. When they get hot enough they can start a fire. That's why you have fuses to stand guard.

46

WHY ARE ELECTRIC WIRES COVERED UP?

ELECTRICITY is very useful as long as we don't get in its way. But it can make trouble for us if we do. Luckily we have a way of avoiding it. We can wrap electrical wires in coats of rubber or plastic. These coats are called insulation. Electricity can't travel through a coat of insulation, and so it runs along safely inside the wire.

If a current of electricity runs through you, it gives you a shock and strong shocks are dangerous. They can kill you. So it is safest not to meddle with electric wires or machines. An electrician knows how to work with electricity, and he doesn't get hurt. Usually he turns a switch so that no current at all comes into the wire on which he is working.

WHY DOES GLUE STICK THINGS TOGETHER?

IN ORDER to see how glue works, we have to know what glue really is. Like everything else in the world, glue is made up of many tiny separate bits called molecules. Each molecule works somewhat like a magnet. It pulls the neighboring glue molecules toward it. We say it attracts them. A glue molecule also attracts the molecules of paper and wood and other materials. This attraction becomes very strong when the glue gets dry. The molecules pull hard on each other and on the materials that need to be held together, and so it makes them stick tight.

There are different kinds of glue. The molecules of some kinds attract wood or paper. Other kinds attract china or glass. Still others work well on almost all materials.

The kind of glue called mucilage is made from the hoofs and horns of animals. Model airplane "dope" is a liquid plastic. Rubber cement comes from rubber, and there is a milky white kind of glue that really is made from milk.

HOW DO WORDS TRAVEL
OVER A TELEPHONE WIRE?

PERHAPS you've made a tin can telephone like the one in the picture. You hold one can and a friend holds the other, with the string stretched tight between. Now let's see what happens when you talk.

First, your voice makes the air move in little waves inside the can. The sound waves strike the bottom of your tin phone and make it move in and out. This movement is called vibration. The vibration of the tin can makes the string vibrate. The vibrating string makes the bottom of the other tin can move in and out. The second tin can pushes against the air and makes sound waves. The sound waves strike your friend's ear, and he hears what you are saying.

A real telephone is something like a toy phone, but it works by electricity. Electric current runs through the wire between your house and a friend's house. The current runs steadily if nothing disturbs it. But let's see what happens when you begin to talk.

Your voice makes sound waves which hit a little round plate in the mouthpiece of the phone.

The little plate vibrates, just as the tin can did. But the plate is connected with the telephone wire in a special way. When the plate vibrates, it makes the electric current travel unevenly.

The uneven current travels to your friend's receiver. There it works an electric magnet. The magnet makes another little plate move in and out. This vibrating receiver plate causes sound waves which travel to your friend's ear. And so he hears what you are saying.

WHAT MAKES A BOOMERANG COME BACK?

A BOOMERANG looks like a jet airplane's wing without the airplane body. This wing shape makes it possible for the boomerang to fly through the air. As it flies, it whirls. Whirling things behave in special ways. A whirling gyroscope top, for example, doesn't fall over. No matter how you tilt it, it continues to go round and round, and in addition its upper tip also moves in a circle.

In the same way a boomerang whirls while it moves in a circle and comes back to the thrower. A boomerang is a combination airplane wing and gyroscope.

Long ago the native people of Australia invented boomerangs for hunting. With his flying weapon a hunter could bring down a bird before it suspected that the boomerang wasn't another bird! The come-back type of boomerang is used mostly for fun. Some Australians can throw it so skillfully that it makes four or five circles in the air before it returns to the owner's hand.

In this country Indians sometimes hunted rabbits with their own kind of boomerang. Unlike the Australian boomerang, the Indian boomerang did not return if it missed its goal.

WHY DO WE FEEL PAIN WHEN WE GET HURT?

SUPPOSE you fall down and bang your elbow and scrape the skin off a knee. Immediately you know that those places hurt. It is as if messages had flashed to your brain, like signals on a telegraph wire: "Elbow aches!" "Knee stings!"

Messages really did travel to your brain, not through wires but through long, thin living threads called nerve cells. Most of the time your pain nerve cells are quiet. But they get excited when something bumps or scrapes them. Then off goes a message to the brain. Your body has several million pain nerve cells. They are closer together in some places than in others. That is why a whack on the nose hurts worse than a slap on the thigh. Doctors don't know exactly how a nerve cell works when it is excited. They do know that chemical changes happen all along the line, and the changes happen very fast. Pain signals travel to your brain at a speed of about 200 miles an hour! No wonder you yell "Ouch!" only a split second after you're hurt.

Why doesn't your hair hurt when it is cut? It doesn't hurt becuse there are no pain nerve cells in a hair. The nerve cells end in the scalp. They send signals when hairs are pulled. But if hair is cut without pulling, the pain nerve cells don't get excited, and so cutting doesn't hurt.

WHAT MAKES RUBBER SNAP BACK?

STRETCH a rubber band till it is long and thin. Then let it go. The band snaps back into its old size and shape. Can you think of anything else that does the same thing? How about a metal spring — the kind that keeps a screen door shut? It stretches out and snaps back, too. Scientists think rubber is made of long molecules in the shape of tiny coiled-up springs.

HOW DOES SOAP MAKE YOU CLEAN?

SOMETIMES it seems like a bother to use soap. But soap really makes you cleaner than plain water does. This is why: There are many small hollows and valleys in your skin. Dirt gets into the hollows and valleys, and there it sticks. Water running over the dirt pushes some of it out. A brush digs some of it out. But soap works differently. It *pulls* dirt away.

When you mix soap with water, wonderful things begin to happen. The soap and water spread out and make bubbles. Each bubble is a little balloon with air inside and a thin skin of soap and water outside. When you make a lather, you are simply pumping air into the soapy water, blowing bubbles.

A soap bubble doesn't seem very strong, but it can pick up dirt. Perhaps you have seen a magnet pick up a tack. Soap bubbles act somewhat like magnets when they pick up dirt. They pull it away from your skin. Soapy lather has many bubbles in it. Each one can pick up a bit of dirt. Then the rinse water carries dirt and bubbles away, and your skin is clean.

Factories make soap from chemicals and oils. In the old days people made their own soap. They made it from wood ashes, water and grease that was left after meat had been cooked. Imagine — ashes get you dirty and grease gets you dirty. But put them together and you have soap to wash the dirt away!

WHAT MAKES STINGING NETTLES STING?

A NETTLE looks like a rather pretty weed. But don't pick it or you will get stung. You will feel as if little needles were jabbing poison into your skin. And that is almost what happens. The nettle plant is covered with tiny, hollow, almost invisible hairs. Each hair works like the needle a doctor uses for injections!

The picture shows how a nettle hair looks under a magnifying glass. A rubbery bulb at the bottom holds the stinging juice. Just a slight touch snaps the tip of the needle, jabs it into your finger and squeezes the juice from the bulb.

Still this disagreeable plant has a use. People in Asia clean off the hairs and break the stems into threads which make good strong cloth.

A nettle sting hurts. But you can stop it easily. Hunt for another kind of weed like the one in the picture. This weed is called dock. Squeeze some dock leaves and dribble the juice on the nettle sting. The pain will soon go away.

The medicine called penicillin is made from a special kind of mold. Scientists grow the mold in tanks in factories.

WHAT MAKES BREAD GET MOLDY?

WHEN BREAD is several days old, you sometimes find little patches of green or gray mold on it. The mold is really a patch of tiny, tiny plants, which grow like weeds in a garden.

Weeds grow wild. Nobody plants them in a garden. Nobody plants mold either. Where does mold come from? It comes from little specks that float around in the air — specks so small that you can't see them. When the specks land on a piece of moist bread in a warm room, they begin to grow, just as seeds grow in warm, moist soil. The tiny mold plants are shaped like flowers, but they are not really flowers. When they have grown, they send out more little specks into the air and onto the bread. The specks are called spores and they are like seeds.

Sometimes mold spores fall onto very dry bread in a very dry room. Then they can't grow. They need moisture, just as all plants do.

Mold grows on other things beside bread. It grows on meat and on vegetables stored in damp places. It grows on the top of home-canned foods that haven't been closed up tight. It can even grow on shoes and clothes and books in damp closets.

53

HOW DO CLOTHES KEEP YOU WARM?

ON A CHILLY DAY you feel as if the cold is coming right through your clothes and hitting your warm skin. But just the opposite really happens. Heat from your body goes out through your clothes. The warmest clothes are the ones that keep heat from escaping.

Heat is a traveler, but it travels through some things more easily than it does through others. You can prove this the next time there is a pot on the stove. Bring your finger close to the pot lid. You feel a lot of heat that has traveled from the gas flame through the metal of the pot. Now feel the black knob on the lid. It is warm but not hot. Heat does not travel through it easily. You can touch it without being burned.

Heat does not travel easily through still air, either. If you could wear a coat of still air, you would be warm, wouldn't you? And that's just what a jacket gives you. It holds a layer of still air near your body. So, when you go out on a chilly day, you really have two coats on, even though you are wearing only one jacket.

Clothes don't need to be heavy in order to keep you warm. Skiers wear under-clothes made of a special kind of net. The holes in the net fill up with air which acts like a blanket.

HOW DOES A FAN MAKE YOU FEEL COOL?

WHEN YOU get very warm, you sweat. Drops of warm water come out of your body through tiny holes in your skin. Most of the drops are very small, and you may not even notice you are sweating. Heat from your body makes these particles of moisture fly off into the air. They evaporate. With each particle that leaves, heat is used up. You feel cooler.

A fan makes sweat evaporate quickly. It creates a little breeze that rushes past you, and the moving air picks up particles of moisture as it goes by. The more air, the more water is picked up and the cooler you are.

HOW DOES AN ELECTRIC REFRIGERATOR WORK?

YOU CAN DO some refrigerating if you put a drop of perfume or shaving lotion or liquid vanilla flavor on the tip of your nose. In a moment or two the liquid dries away into the air, and the spot on your nose feels much cooler. We say that the liquid evaporated. When liquids evaporate they carry heat away with them.

Inside your kitchen refrigerator a special liquid in a long metal pipe does the cooling job. The liquid, called freon, evaporates very fast, and so it makes things cold very quickly. It travels around and around in the pipe, so it can be used over and over.

The freon travels first to the part of the refrigerator that holds the food. There it evaporates. Then, carrying heat with it, it goes on through the pipe, out of the refrigerator box, to a radiator where it gets rid of the heat it collected inside the box. Now the freon is ready to return and carry away more heat, keeping the refrigerator cold.

The electric machinery in the refrigerator runs a pump that pushes the freon around and around through the pipe.

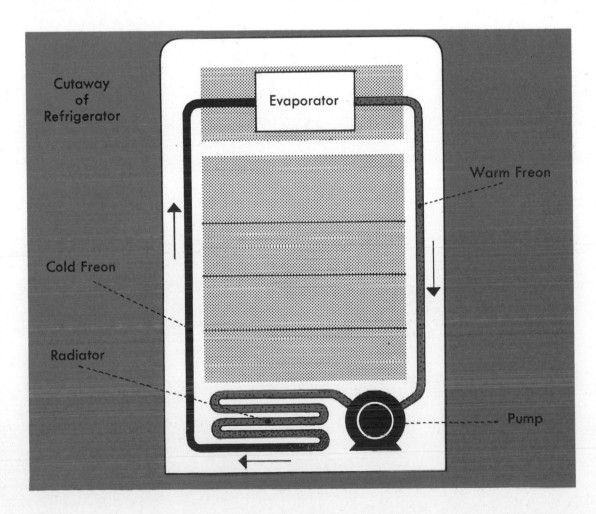

THESE GERMS are tiny living plants called bacteria. Like all living things they eat and grow. They can take what they need to eat from our bodies, and they grow very quickly. Each full-grown one can divide into two new bacteria. Then these two split, making four. Soon there are millions of them. All these millions of bacteria act like little factories which produce chemicals of different kinds. Some of the chemicals are poisonous. And so they make us sick.

Our bodies can manufacture chemicals, too, and some of our chemicals can kill harmful bacteria. Medicines kill others.

Another kind of germ is called a virus. Doctors still do not know exactly how a virus works, but they have invented wonderful medicines that keep some kinds of virus from harming us.

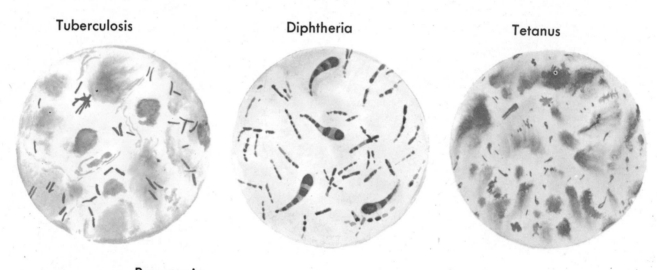

Tuberculosis   **Diphtheria**   **Tetanus**

Pneumonia

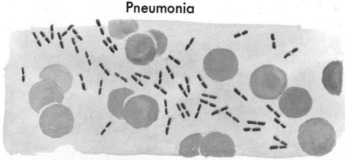

This is the way bacteria look when they are magnified by a microscope. If you looked at a virus through the same microscope, you couldn't see it at all, because it is so tiny. Scientists must use a specially powerful instrument called an electron microscope to find out what a virus looks like.

56

Rabies germs make animals and people sick. A bite passes the germ along from skunk to dog and from dog to man. Injections can protect your pets and you from rabies.

HOW DOES VACCINATION WORK?

WHEN THE doctor vaccinates you, he makes a little scratch on your skin. Then he squeezes a drop of liquid onto the scratch and rubs it in. Later the spot may feel a little sore. This one small sore spot is a sign that your whole body can now protect itself against germs which cause a disease called smallpox.

Your body fights a battle against many kinds of germs all the time. Usually it wins. That is why you stay well. Your body protects itself with various weapons. Sometimes it makes a substance that seems to paralyze the germs. Another substance dissolves them. Another makes the germs clump together so that they can't harm you.

But sometimes a strong kind of germ can take your body by surprise. It wins out for a while, and you feel sick. Your body has to work hard conquering these germs. Often, when the fight is won, that same kind of germ can not make you sick again.

Now suppose your body could have practice in winning battles. Suppose it could fight some weak germs before it had to battle against strong ones of the same kind. Would this give it the power to conquer the strong ones before they could make you sick? The answer is yes. That is what happens when you get vaccinated. Weak germs floating in liquid enter your body through the scratch the doctor makes. These weak germs give your body practice in making a weapon to use against strong smallpox germs. If the smallpox germs enter your body later on, they cannot make you sick.

WHAT IS ATOMIC ENERGY?

WHEN a piece of wood burns, it gives off heat and light. Scientists say that heat and light are forms of energy. Left alone, wood doesn't give off heat and light. We have to kindle a fire, and there has to be plenty of oxygen so that the fire can burn. The same is true of coal and other fuels. But there are certain substances that act quite differently. They give off energy all by themselves, without any outside help. Two of these special substances are radium and uranium. They are made of atoms which behave differently from the atoms of most other substances.

An atom, you probably know, is the smallest possible bit of a substance. Now most atoms go on and on being themselves, never changing. But radium and uranium atoms are different. Every so often, one of them will suddenly fly apart. It gives off a tiny spark of light and a bit of heat. We call this atomic energy because it comes from atoms that fly apart.

In a piece of uranium ore the atoms break up one after another, not very fast, in a hit-or-miss way, and the energy goes to waste. To use this atomic energy, scientists have invented ways of controlling the rate at which the atoms give up their heat. In an atomic plant, the heat is used to make steam which turns generators and produces electricity.

In an atomic bomb the energy of a great many atoms is released very fast — in about a millionth of a second. This makes a violent explosion. In addition to heat, the atoms give off particles of electricity and very powerful X-rays. This is called radiation, and it is terribly dangerous. The people who work with atomic energy take great care to protect themselves from radiation. They keep the uranium and other radioactive materials in special containers from which most of the rays can't escape. Although bombs and radiation have done much harm, scientists have also learned how to put radiation to good use. Radioactive medicines help doctors cure diseases. Other radioactive materials help to give us better food, fewer insects, safer automobile parts. One atomic gadget can even make sure that a tube of toothpaste is full before it goes on sale.

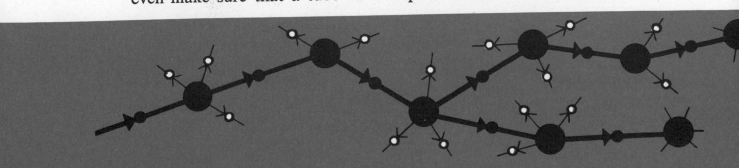

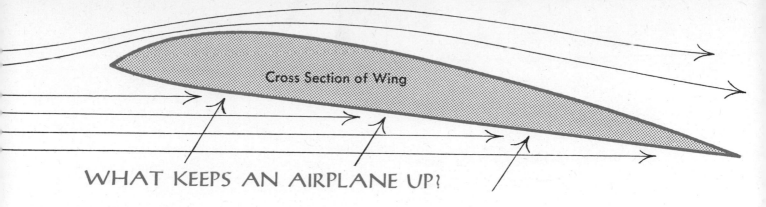

Cross Section of Wing

WHAT KEEPS AN AIRPLANE UP?

AIR KEEPS an airplane from falling. Most of the time you don't feel or see air, and so you forget that it is a real thing, not just empty space. But when air moves fast in a high wind, it pushes against you very hard. You get the same feeling when you drive fast in an open car, although it is you who are moving through the air.

Because air is a definite something, it has weight. Scientists have weighed it, and the figures they've worked out may astonish you. Suppose you hold a sheet of writing paper out level in front of you. More than a thousand pounds of air are pushing down on that piece of paper. How can you possibly hold up that much weight? *You* aren't holding it up. Air holds it up, because air pushes on the paper from all sides. There is an upward push of a thousand pounds that equals the downward push.

Now think about an airplane wing, which is much wider and longer than a piece of paper. Since air pushes against every inch of the wing, you can see that the pressure is enormous. But nothing happens because the downward and the upward push of air are equal.

Would something happen if you could somehow take away pressure so that there would be less downward push? Of course! If you made the downward push small enough, the upward push would lift the plane into the air. But how could that be done? Inventors have discovered that the secret is to make the airplane wing in a special shape. The curved top surface is longer than the straight bottom surface. Now when the wing moves through the air, pressure on the long top surface decreases. But pressure on the bottom stays the same, or it may even increase if the wing is tilted a little. As the plane moves faster, there is more and more and more difference in the pressure on the two sides of the wing. At last the upward push is enough to hold the whole weight of the plane. It leaves the ground. It flies because air is keeping it up.

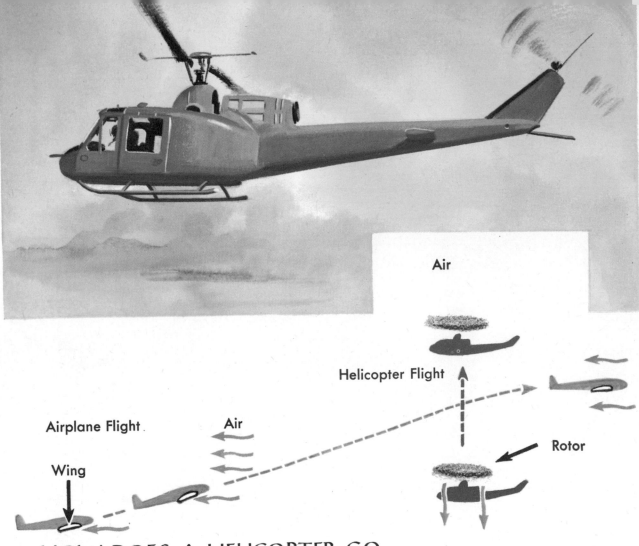

Air

Helicopter Flight

Airplane Flight

Air

Wing

Rotor

HOW DOES A HELICOPTER GO STRAIGHT UP IN THE AIR?

A HELICOPTER doesn't seem to have any wing. Instead it has a rotor that whirls round and round above the body of the machine. Actually the rotor is a wing. It lifts the helicopter just the way an airplane wing lifts the plane.

An airplane has to get up speed before it can rise off the ground. It rolls along a runway, faster and faster, until its wing is moving through the air quickly enough for it to take off. A helicopter wing — that is, the rotor — also has to go faster and faster before the copter can take off. But the rotor goes faster and faster *in a circle,* while the body of the copter stays in place. Soon the whirling rotor-wing is moving quickly enough to take off. It lifts evenly, and the body of the copter follows, almost straight up.

60

YOU TURN ON the radio and a program comes to you from a broadcasting station miles and miles away. You know that words and music themselves haven't traveled all that distance through space, but something certainly is bringing the program from the station. What is this silent carrier of sound?

The answer is radio waves. You can't see radio waves, or feel them or even hear them. In fact, nobody knows exactly what they are. But we do know that they are made by electricity, and we have learned how to use them.

At the broadcasting station people talk or sing, instruments play, doors slam, and all of these make sound waves. The sound waves reach the microphone, and here they are changed into electricity. Then from a tall tower called the broadcasting antenna, electricity sends out radio waves. The waves travel in every direction, and some of them reach your radio antenna. Now a wonderful thing happens. The radio waves start an electric current in your antenna like the one that was first made in the broadcasting station. Finally, the loudspeaker in your set changes electricity into sound, and you hear the program.

HOW DOES TELEVISION WORK?

TELEVISION uses the same kind of wonderful invisible, soundless waves that make your radio work. At the broadcasting station, a special camera picks up light waves while the microphone picks up sound waves. Both are changed to electricity. Electricity makes the television waves which bring the program to your set, where it becomes sound and light to make the picture on the screen.

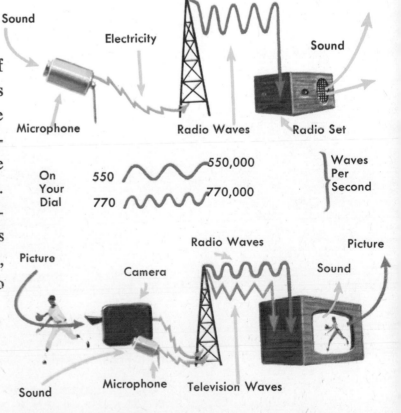

Sound · Electricity · Sound
Microphone · Radio Waves · Radio Set

On Your Dial · 550 · 550,000 · 770 · 770,000 · Waves Per Second

Picture · Camera · Radio Waves · Picture · Sound
Sound · Microphone · Television Waves

WHAT IS RADAR?

WHEN RADAR was first invented it had a long name — Radio Detecting and Ranging. This was soon shortened and made into a new name by using letters from each of the words *RAdio Detecting And Ranging*.

With radar, men can look through fog and darkness. For example, radar gives airplane pilots and sea captains special eyes that can see in the blackest night. If you are a ship's captain looking at radar, you see little spots of light called pips on a scope, which is somewhat like a round television screen. Your own ship is shown by a blob of light in the center of the scope. Pips everywhere else on the screen stand for objects all around you. The pips look almost like a map. They warn you about other ships or icebergs or islands or anything else you might bump into. Numbers and letters on the scope tell just how far away these objects are.

A pilot watching a radar scope in his plane can tell where other planes are. And he can locate landing fields, even through clouds and fog and pitch dark.

Radar on the ground can locate planes in the air. It can also detect things far out in space. With radar telescopes scientists have discovered stars that have grown cold and no longer give off the least bit of light!

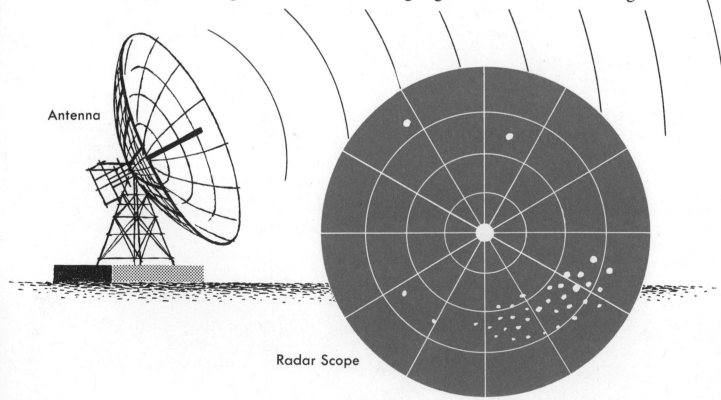

Antenna

Radar Scope

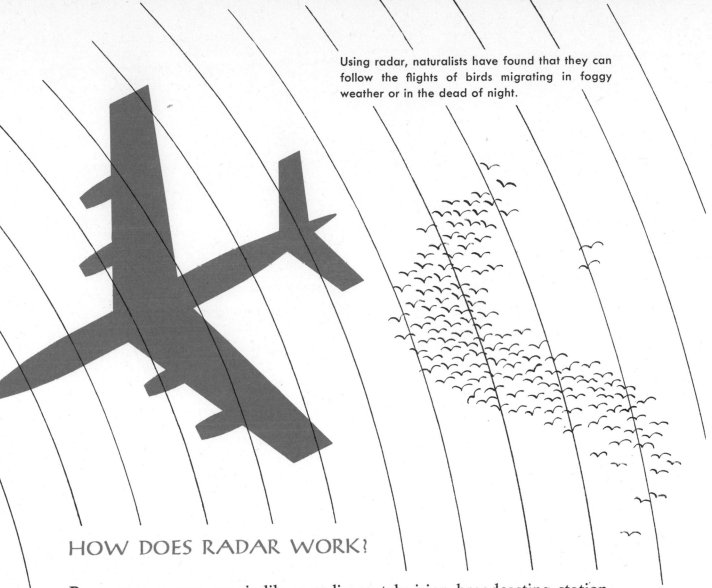

Using radar, naturalists have found that they can follow the flights of birds migrating in foggy weather or in the dead of night.

HOW DOES RADAR WORK?

PART OF A RADAR SET is like a radio or television broadcasting station. It sends out radio waves. When these waves hit solid objects they bounce back. The return waves are picked up by another part of the radar, and this part acts like the television set in your house. It changes the radio waves into light. Bright spots of light, called pips, appear on the radar screen, showing that the waves have hit an object and bounced back from it.

Radio waves travel very fast — about 186,000 miles a second. So radar has to be very quick to keep up with the waves. In a split second it does two things: It measures the time that the waves took traveling out to an object and back again. Then it automatically figures how far away the object is. Instantly a light appears on the screen showing the distance to the object and the direction in which it is located.

WHAT KEEPS THE EARTH
GOING AROUND THE SUN?

PERHAPS YOU have played with a ball tied to a string like the one in the picture. Then you know what happens when you swing the ball around in a big circle. You can feel it tugging at the string. As long as you keep the ball moving, it stays in the air, going round and round.

The earth is something like that ball. It whirls around the sun. But where is the string that holds it? Of course, there isn't a string from earth to sun. But there is something just as real. A strong invisible force pulls the earth toward the sun. This force is the sun's gravity.

The sun pulls the earth, but the earth tugs against the pull — like the ball at the end of a string. The tug of the whirling earth balances the pull of the sun's gravity. And so the earth keeps on a regular path. The earth's path around the sun is called its orbit.

WHY DOES WATER PUT OUT A FIRE?

BEFORE we can answer that question we have to remember that a fire needs air in order to burn. Now what happens when a fireman squirts water on the burning wall of a house? Instantly the heat turns the water to steam. Steam is actually a hot gas that takes up much more space than water. So it bursts outward, away from the wall of the burning house. As it goes, it pushes air away, too. Without air the flames die down.

At the same time water does something else — something much more important than drowning the flames. It cools the burning wall. Cooling is the main thing that puts the fire out. Wood can't burn, even with air around it, unless it is quite hot already. That is why you use a match and paper and small pieces of kindling when you want to burn a big piece of wood in a stove or a fireplace. First the match heats the thin paper, so the paper begins to burn. Flames from the paper heat the kindling, and soon it burns, too. Finally the big stick of wood is hot enough so that it can burn.

CHAPTER IV

How Did They Do It?

YES, it is sometimes possible to make rain. First the rainmaker must have clouds to work on. The best kind are usually the big woolly ones, full of moisture, floating in cool air.

The rainmaker flies over the clouds in an airplane and "seeds" them from above. That means he sprays them with chemicals or with powdered dry ice. The tiny particles of chemical or dry ice float around in the clouds and offer a kind of platform for moisture to cling to. More and more moisture gathers around these particles. At last they are too heavy to float, and so they fall to earth. They are man-made rain.

HOW COULD PEOPLE BUILD THE PYRAMIDS WITHOUT BIG MACHINES?

LONG, LONG AGO, before cranes or elevators were invented, the kings of Egypt had great tombs built for themselves. These tombs, the pyramids, were made of enormous stone blocks. Unless you know the trick, it seems impossible for men without big machines to stack the blocks up one on top of the other.

This is what the pyramid builders did: They set the bottom layer of stones in place. Then they built a gently sloping road that led up onto this first layer. Next they hauled more stones, one by one, up the sloping road and set a second layer in place. Now they added onto the road so that it reached the top of the second layer. Again they dragged stones up the slope to build the third layer. And so, over and over, they raised the road for each row of stones. When the last block was in place, they cleared the road completely away.

The Egyptians used no wagons or animals to haul their stones. They had only human muscle-power and wooden rollers. Men, pulling on ropes attached to wooden platforms, rolled the heavy loads across the desert and up the slopes. The Great Pyramid, built 4,500 years ago, is nearly 500 feet high, and it took about 100,000 people altogether to do the work.

WHERE DOES RUBBER COME FROM?

THE TOUGH, firm tire on your bike was once a liquid, and that liquid was sap in a tree — a rubber tree. In order to get the rubber sap, which is called latex, men had to cut slits in the tree bark and let the milky liquid flow out into buckets. The latex was then dried and hardened and sent to rubber factories. There men cooked it and mixed it with chemicals and turned it into the various kinds of rubber that we use every day.

Rubber now comes mostly from trees grown in southern Asia, but

Here are some other things that the Indians invented: Hammock — The sailors on Columbus' ships were the first Europeans to see hammocks in Indian houses.

Snowshoes and toboggans — The Indians of New York and Canada discovered that these two inventions made it easier to travel over snowy country.

the first home of the rubber tree was South America. Long before Columbus crossed the Atlantic Ocean, Indians discovered how to make latex into rubber boots. First an Indian bootmaker would take some mud and model it into a foot. This he fastened to a stick. Next he dipped the mud foot into a dish of latex, dried it over a smoky fire, and dipped it again. Layer by layer he built up a thick coating of smoked rubber. Finally, when it was thick enough, he had only to soak out the mud and put on a waterproof boot.

South American Indians also invented the idea of playing games with rubber balls.

Canoes — Although people in many parts of the world made dugout canoes, the Indians invented the narrow-ended canoe made of a light frame covered with bark.

MORE THAN 5,000 years ago, in a country called Sumeria, the priests had many responsibilities. They had to keep track of how much grain was put away in huge storehouses. They had to remember how much of it should be saved for seed. They had to know how many bricks it would take to build a new temple and how many men would be needed to lay the bricks.

All of this got to be too much for priests just to keep in their heads. Besides, if the one who knew about the seed grain died, there might not be enough saved to plant the fields the following year. Something had to be done.

The priests needed a way to store up information so they could get it when they wanted it. To solve their problem, someone invented the idea of making marks on thin bricks made of damp clay. Each mark would have a meaning that all the priests agreed to. There would be marks for numbers and marks for things. When the damp bricks or tablets were dried, the marks would remain. Any priest could then look at the tablets, and he would know how many measures of grain, for example, another priest had entered in his records.

This was the way writing began.

The oldest writing in the world was picture-writing. The word for *man* was a drawing of a man. But after a while people drew the words more simply. Finally the words were nothing more than squiggles. Alphabets and the idea of spelling out words were invented long after picture-writing. Before the invention of printing machines and typewriters, everything had to be written by hand. Monks often spent their whole time making beautiful copies of books.

WHY IS MILK HOMOGENIZED?

MILK IS HOMOGENIZED to save you the trouble of shaking the bottle when you want to mix milk and cream together. Ordinary whole milk separates into skim milk and cream. Homogenized milk does not.

This is how homogenized milk is made: The dairy man pours ordinary milk into a tank. Then the milk is forced out of the tank through very tiny holes. This simple process makes the cream stay mixed with the rest of the milk.

Homogenized milk and ordinary whole milk have exactly the same amount of nourishment.

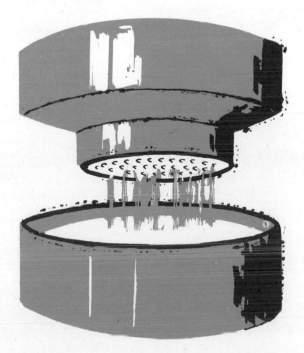

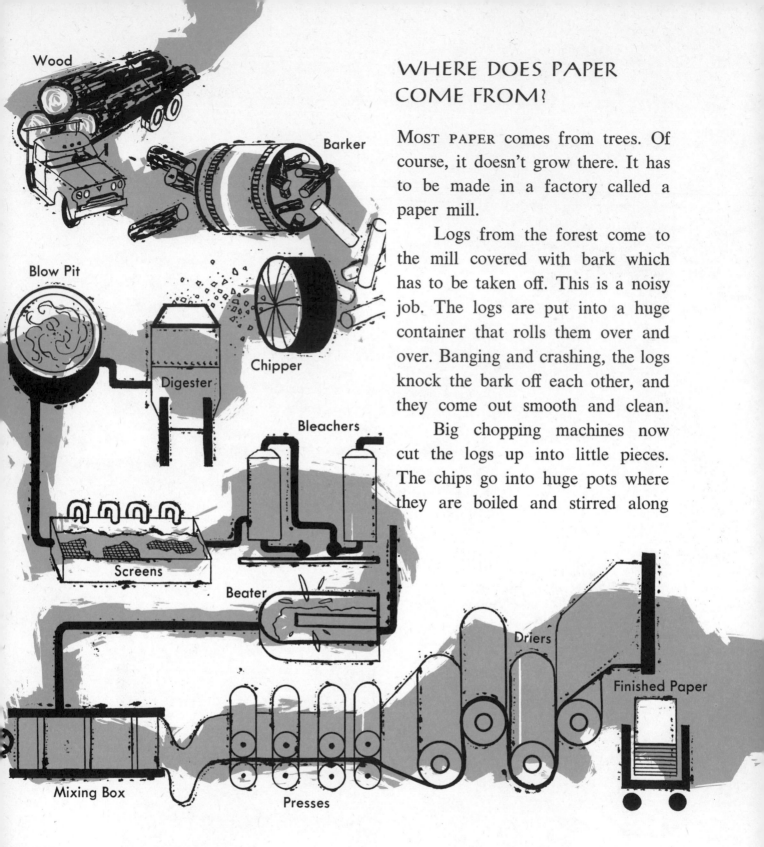

Wood

Barker

Blow Pit

Chipper

Digester

Bleachers

Screens

Beater

Driers

Finished Paper

Mixing Box

Presses

WHERE DOES PAPER COME FROM?

MOST PAPER comes from trees. Of course, it doesn't grow there. It has to be made in a factory called a paper mill.

Logs from the forest come to the mill covered with bark which has to be taken off. This is a noisy job. The logs are put into a huge container that rolls them over and over. Banging and crashing, the logs knock the bark off each other, and they come out smooth and clean.

Big chopping machines now cut the logs up into little pieces. The chips go into huge pots where they are boiled and stirred along with strong chemicals until the wood turns soft and the mixture is mushy.

Next the mush goes through giant wringers that dry it and let it settle into thin sheets. To make paper very white, men at the mill use bleach just the way your mother uses bleach when she washes white clothes.

The paper you write letters on sometimes has chopped-up rags in it as well as wood. The rags make it smooth and strong. When you sell old clothes to the junk man, he sells some of them to the paper mill. Maybe the postman brought you a piece of somebody's worn-out shirt in the mail today.

Before paper was invented, ancient Egyptians wrote on papyrus which they made from a plant called the papyrus reed. First they removed the outer bark of the reeds. Then they took off thin sheets of filmy stuff which they glued together in layers, using flour paste. Another ancient writing material was parchment. This came from specially scraped and cured sheepskins or goatskins. Vellum was a very white and fine writing material made from the skins of calves less than six weeks old.

HOW DID PEOPLE LEARN TO TALK?

HUMAN BEINGS have special muscles in their tongues. No other animals have these muscles. Tongue muscles are controlled by one particular part of the brain, and this part is bigger in human beings than in any other animal. The result of these two facts is that people can make more different kinds of sound than any other creatures can make. Of course, babies aren't born knowing how to make sense with all these sounds. They must learn to talk. And language had to be invented first.

Maybe the first words anyone spoke were imitations of the sounds people heard around them—sounds like *buzz, pop, snap*. Most likely people started to talk because they felt they just *had* to say things to each other. Nobody really knows how talking began, but all it needed was a start. A few people agreed that a few sounds would have certain meanings, and then they could use these first words to help them make others. The fashion of talking spread rapidly. Possibly speech was invented several different times in several different parts of the world. At any rate, there are about 3,000 different languages spoken on earth today.

WHERE DOES SALT COME FROM?

SALT COMES from mines, from wells, from springs, from salt lakes, and from the sea.

The tunnels and rooms of a salt mine sparkle as if they had been dug through ice. Miners, using drills, cut the solid salt away in great glistening chunks. Then power shovels scoop it up and load it into little railroad cars which haul it out of the mine.

A salt well is very different from an ordinary well. It is a hole in the ground all right, but pumps force water down *into* it! This water dissolves salt which is buried in the earth. Then the salty water, called brine, is pumped back out and boiled in pans. The water evaporates, leaving the salt in the pans.

Sometimes an underground stream flows through a bed of salt. When it comes to the surface it is a salt spring. Brine from these springs and from salt lakes and from the sea, can be boiled to make salt. More often, the naturally salty water is allowed to stand in the sun in big shallow reservoirs or ponds. The sun dries the water away, and the salt stays behind.

In the old days salt was scarce. Only those people who lived near the sea could get it easily. But everybody needed it to preserve meat and fish because they had no refrigerators in those days. Salt was so valuable that it was used as money in some places.

CHEWING GUM comes from the juice of bully-trees, which grow in steamy hot jungles in Central America. Men climb into the trees and make cuts in the trunks. Soon the milky white juice begins to ooze out and trickle along the cuts, down into buckets on the ground.

Now the men start fires and cook the juice in big pots. When it gets thick and rubbery, they cool it and shape it into cakes as big as pillows. This rubbery stuff is called chicle, and it is ready to travel, first on mule-back, then by boat, to a chewing gum factory in our country.

At the factory the chicle is cooked again. Special machines stir sugar and flavoring into the gum and knead it like dough until at last it is ready to be rolled out and cut into sticks for you to chew.

Bubble gum comes from chicle like other chewing gum, but it has a special kind of plastic mixed in it. This plastic is soft and stretchy. In fact, it is a kind of artificial rubber made from chemicals. The rubbery stuff stretches out into a very thin film when you blow on it, and that's how bubble gum makes bubbles.

HOW DO THEY GET WILD ANIMALS FOR THE CIRCUS AND THE ZOO?

A WILD ANIMAL collector first has to learn about the animals he wants to catch. He studies books. He talks to people who live in the forests or jungles or deserts where the animals live. He learns the tricks that these people have used in capturing wild beasts. Then, after he has watched the animals, he invents a few tricks of his own. One African bird collector made himself an ostrich costume. Wearing it he could walk into a flock of ostriches without rousing their suspicion. Then he'd lasso a big bird.

GLASS is made of sand — clean white sand. Men at the glass factory melt the sand in a furnace till it looks like thick sugar syrup. Of course, they need a much, much hotter fire than the fire in your kitchen stove. Usually they add soda and chalk which help the sand to melt into clear glass.

Many things can be done with hot, syrupy glass. For windowpanes, glassmakers pour out glass and machines roll it into big sheets of just the right thickness. To make dishes and drinking glasses, they pour the liquid glass into molds. The man in the picture is blowing a glass bubble which he will shape into a beautiful bowl. Milk bottles and pop bottles are made by machines which blow and mold the glass at the same time into the right shapes.

Safety glass for automobiles is really a sandwich made from two slices of glass with a clear plastic filling between. The plastic holds the glass so tight that it can't splinter off and cut you if it is cracked or broken.

Melted glass can also be spun into silky fibers and woven into cloth which doesn't catch fire the way ordinary cloth does. Fiber glass makes good curtains for homes and theaters and ships.

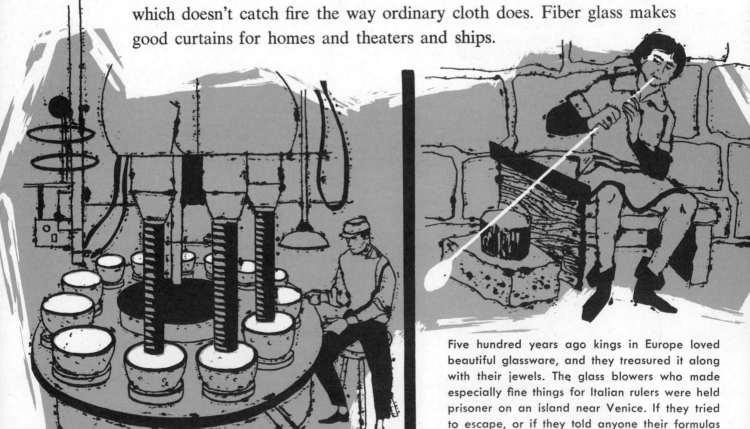

Five hundred years ago kings in Europe loved beautiful glassware, and they treasured it along with their jewels. The glass blowers who made especially fine things for Italian rulers were held prisoner on an island near Venice. If they tried to escape, or if they told anyone their formulas for making glass, the punishment was death.

CHAPTER V

Information Please

WHAT MAKES SODA POP FIZZ?

THE BUBBLY stuff in soda pop is a gas, but not the same kind of gas that burns in your kitchen stove. The gas in soda pop will not burn at all.

As long as you let a bottle of pop sit still, the gas stays mixed up with the flavored water. But if you jiggle the bottle, tiny bubbles of gas start to rise up. They are lighter than the water, so they float to the top. When you take the cap off the bottle, they keep on rising. More bubbles follow. They come out so fast that they bring some of the pop along with them in a frothy foam. The bubbles are like little balloons. When they burst they make a fizzing sound.

ARE MERMAIDS REAL?

BEAUTIFUL MERMAID ladies with scaly fish tails are found only in fairy stories. Just the same, sailors and travelers used to believe absolutely that they had seen the "ladies of the sea." (That's what *mermaid* means.)

Real creatures called manatees probably caused the mermaid legends. These animals live in the ocean, and since they are mammals, not fish, they have to come up for air. Like all mammals, the mother manatee feeds her baby milk, and like human mothers she often cradles the baby, holding it with a flipper while it nurses. Manatees also pop out of the water unexpectedly and pause for a while in an upright position as if standing on their tails.

You can imagine that sailors might think a manatee was half-human, particularly if it was far from the ship — or if the day was foggy or the sailor nearsighted.

A manatee is also called a sea cow.

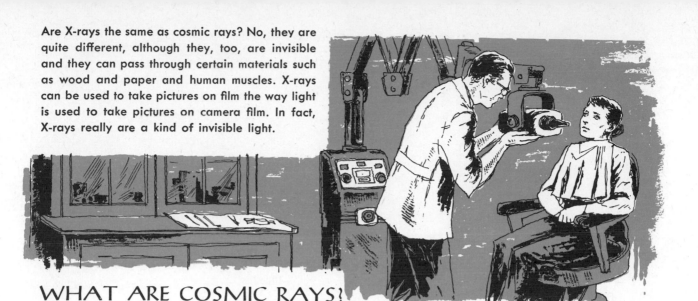

Are X-rays the same as cosmic rays? No, they are quite different, although they, too, are invisible and they can pass through certain materials such as wood and paper and human muscles. X-rays can be used to take pictures on film the way light is used to take pictures on camera film. In fact, X-rays really are a kind of invisible light.

WHAT ARE COSMIC RAYS?

FOR A LONG TIME scientists wondered about something they called cosmic rays. They could see the tracks of cosmic rays. Instruments in laboratories could measure them. But nobody knew what the rays themselves were. If an experimenter happened to have a glass jar full of vapor from water or alcohol, he could watch cosmic rays at work. The rays would zip right through the glass, hit the cloudy vapor, and leave a trail behind. These powerful rays seemed to come from outer space at tremendous speeds, and they could pass through glass and metal, even through stone walls.

Now the mystery has been solved. We know that a cosmic ray is simply the heavy center of an atom. Its real name is the *nucleus* of the atom. Some cosmic rays are formed in the sun and shot out into space. Many of them reach the earth. Others remain in the air high above the earth.

You can imagine how a cosmic ray is made if you think of a peach caught up in a tornado. The powerful wind rips off the fuzz and the skin and the yellow fruit till only the seed remains. Finally the wind hurls the seed off like a bullet.

Tornadoes of glowing gas whirl over the sun's surface all the time. They strip away the outside parts of atoms, leaving only the center parts. Then the stripped-down atoms are flung off. Some of them are still traveling like bullets when they hit the walls of buildings on earth.

Scientists feel quite sure that cosmic rays must have some effect upon the earth and even on human beings, but they still don't know exactly what those effects are and nobody really knows where they all come from.

THE SUN looks like a great ball of fire. It is really a ball of gases so hot that it glows with a bright light. Most of the gas in the sun is hydrogen. Some of it is helium. The sun also contains many of the other substances that we have here on earth — for example, iron and nickel. On earth these metals are solid, the way ice is solid. You know what happens when ice is heated. It turns to water and finally to a hot gas that we call steam. The sun is so hot that the metals in it are not solid or even liquid. They are gases instead!

WHAT ARE ATOMS MADE OF?

AN ATOM of gold or silver or uranium is the smallest possible bit of gold or silver or uranium. It is so tiny that you couldn't even see it with the strongest microscope. People used to think that atoms were little round solid pills, the littlest things in the world. But scientists have discovered that an atom can be divided. In all atoms there are tiny particles of electricity called electrons. Atoms have other particles in them, too, and scientists still haven't found out all about them.

A particle of electricity is really a particle of energy. So we can say that an atom is really made of energy!

WHY DID THE INDIANS USE BOWS AND ARROWS?

BOWS AND ARROWS were the best weapons in the world until guns were invented. Indians developed great skill in killing game and enemies with the arrowheads they made from stone. When the first Spanish soldiers came to America with Columbus, many white men used bows, but they had metal arrowheads, and they wore metal armor for protection. These gave the Spaniards an advantage, but more important were the guns which all white men used before long.

With guns the white invaders defeated the Indians in battle after battle, in war after war. The Indians never had a chance to learn how to manufacture the powerful weapons for themselves.

Before Indians learned how to use the bow and arrow, their deadliest weapon was the spear, which they threw hard and far with the help of a spear thrower. This gadget served as an extra joint in the arm of the hunter or warrior.

WHAT IS A ROCKOON?

"ROCKOON" is a new word. Weathermen made it up a few years ago to describe a new invention of theirs. A rockoon is a combination rocket and balloon, which carries measuring instruments high into the air. First the balloon goes up about 15 miles above the earth. Then the rocket automatically shoots off and climbs another 45 miles. An automatic radio in the rocket sends back messages about the atmosphere — about its temperature, about winds, about radiation far above the earth. This kind of information helps scientists to understand more about weather. It also helps astronauts to build safer machines for space travel.

HOW DOES ICE MAKE THINGS COLD?

WHEN YOU TOUCH a piece of ice, your finger feels cold. It feels as if the cold is creeping from the ice into your finger. But really it is the other way around. Heat from your finger has gone out into the ice. That heat melts a little of the ice and turns it to water. You can feel the water on your finger.

Now suppose you put a little piece of ice into a glass of orange juice. The ice takes some of the heat from the juice. As it takes the heat away, the ice turns into water. The piece of ice gets smaller and smaller, and the juice gets cooler and cooler. Ice cools all kinds of things by taking heat out of them.

Do you know how to keep a piece of ice from melting fast? Wrap it in a blanket. That may sound silly, but it isn't. When you leave a piece of ice unwrapped, warm air keeps moving around it. And the ice keeps taking more and more heat out of the air. So it melts quickly. But a blanket protects the ice from moving air. The wrapped-up ice melts more slowly.

WHY DO TREES LOSE THEIR LEAVES IN FALL?

ALL SPRING and summer the leaves on a tree do an important job. They act like little food factories manufacturing food for the living tree. To do this they need air and water, sunshine and minerals from the soil.

Water comes to the leaves up the tree trunk from the roots. Roots get water from soil around them. Leaves breathe air in and out through tiny holes that you can see only with a microscope. When they breathe out, they give off invisible droplets of water at the same time.

All summer long the little leaf-factories work at making food for the tree. But in fall, when there is less sunlight, they stop. The tree has already stored up enough food to last through the winter. Now it rests — the way a bear rests when it goes to sleep in a hollow log or a cave after cold weather comes.

Just before the tree starts to rest it corks up all the little holes at the base of the leaves through which water has been coming. It makes a bit of real cork, and this tough waterproof stuff actually pushes each leaf off as it grows. The leaves fall, and that's why we often call autumn "the fall."

If trees didn't cork up the water tubes, the leaves would keep on breathing out water, even after the ground was frozen. But roots can't take water out of frozen ground. And so, if water kept disappearing, the inside of the tree would dry out and it would die.

DO PLANTS GO TO SLEEP AT NIGHT?

SLEEP is probably not the right word to use when we talk about plants. Animals sleep but there are important differences between animals and plants. Still, plants do change when the sun goes down. They are not the same at night as in the daytime. When sunlight disappears they stop making food for themselves just as if they were resting or sleeping.

WHAT GOOD IS GRAVITY?

YOU HAVE probably heard that space travelers can easily pick up huge rocks when they land on Mars. That is because gravity on Mars does not pull as strongly as gravity on earth. If gravity makes it hard to lift things, wouldn't it be better if we had less of it? How would life be if gravity pulled much less than it now does?

Take the space traveler first of all. If he had grown up with less gravity on earth, he wouldn't find it so easy to lift big stones on Mars. The reason? He developed muscles by lifting things against the pull of gravity. You do the same thing every time you chin yourself, or jump, or climb the stairs or even lift a tennis racket. You are fighting against gravity. The work your muscles do in this fight makes them strong.

If gravity suddenly grew less on earth, we would have bodies that were much stronger than we needed. This might not be so terrible, but another thing would be. We wouldn't have enough air to breathe. Air is very light, and it would fly off into space if gravity didn't keep pulling it toward the earth.

Inventors make gravity work for us in many ways. Here are a few of them:

A swing. Your muscles pump the swing upward. Gravity brings it swooping down.

Water supply. Gravity pulls water down from the reservoir, through pipes and into your house.

Electricity. Water, pulled by gravity, turns a wheel. The wheel turns a generator which sends electric current through wires to your house.

Here is a clever gravity machine. It is a water clock that kept time in an Egyptian palace more than two thousand years ago. The statue is connected to a water pipe. Water from the pipe, pulled by gravity, comes out of the eyes of the statue like tears. These tears drop — gravity again — into a basin. From the basin — again pulled by gravity — water drips at a steady rate into a bottle. In the bottle is a stool with a small figure of a man sitting on it. The man points at numbers that correspond to the hours of the day. As the dripping water gradually fills the bottle, it lifts the stool and the figure. The pointing hand rises steadily higher minute by minute, hour by hour, indicating the time as it goes up. After twelve hours the bottle drains and the clock starts over again. (Based on Lancelot Hogben.)

85

IS THERE GOLD IN THE SEA?

THE SEA has more gold than any mine in the world. There is ninety million dollars' worth of gold in every cubic mile of sea water. (You can imagine a cubic mile of water if you think of filling a tank a mile wide, a mile long, and a mile deep.) But nobody has ever got rich mining sea gold. The cost of separating it from the water is much greater than the gold itself is worth. So it's much more sensible to fish in the ocean for good things to eat!

WHAT ARE THE CLOUDS?

WHITE CLOUDS, pink clouds, gray clouds — all clouds are made of the same thing. They are all made of water. Each drop of water in a cloud is so small that it can float in the air. It is so small that you wouldn't notice it all by itself. But when many of these drops come close together you can see them. They form a cloud.

Most clouds float high up in the air. But sometimes they gather near the ground. Then you can walk around inside a cloud, and you say it is foggy weather. A fog is really a cloud that forms very close to the ground.

WHAT IS THE SMALLEST ANIMAL?

THE VERY smallest creatures in the world can be seen only if you look at them through a microscope. The smallest furry animal is a fat-tailed shrew. It is very fragile. You can break its bones just by picking it up. This little animal may also hold another record. It is probably the biggest eater. For its size it gobbles up more food than any other four-footed creature. Every day its tiny sharp teeth chew through a pile of food weighing two and a half times as much as it weighs. Imagine doing that yourself. If you weigh sixty pounds, you would have to eat, in *one* day, 150 loaves of bread or about three pillowcases full of oatmeal. Or, if you prefer chocolate bars, you'd have to eat ten stacks of them, and each stack would be about four feet high!

IS A TEPEE THE SAME AS A WIGWAM?

INDIANS who used to live along the east coast of the United States built houses called wigwams. A wigwam was shaped like half an orange, with the flat side down, and it was covered with sheets of bark or bundles of reeds. These were materials which the Indians found along river banks or in the woods. When they moved, they always left their wigwams behind and built new ones in new places.

Tepees were the homes of Indians who lived on the Great Plains. A tepee was made of poles and animal skins, shaped like a cone with the flat side down. Tepees could be moved and put up in different places.

Pueblo Indians in the Southwest made square houses of mud or stone piled one on top of the other. A Pueblo village was really one big apartment house.

Many Navaho Indians today live in hogans — six-sided houses made of logs and mud.

In warm Florida the Indians built houses without walls. Since they lived in swampy places they put their homes on platforms on stilts.

Indians on the Northwest coast lived in houses that looked like big barns built of boards that they split from great trees in the forests nearby.

CRICKETS, butterflies, ladybugs, ants — all of them disappear in the fall. But when warm weather comes in spring you see them again. Where have they been?

Cool weather sends a cricket scurrying to the little underground nest he has built for himself. There he sleeps all winter. We say he hibernates. Some other insects hibernate, too.

The orange and black monarch butterflies move away to warmer country when autumn weather grows cold. Great flocks of monarchs fly away together. They are migrating. Ladybugs migrate, too.

Ants behave the way people do. They stay in their snug homes part of the time and come out into the sunshine when it is warm.

Most grown-up insects die at the end of summer. But they leave large numbers of eggs. The eggs will hatch in spring when all kinds of things in nature make a new beginning.

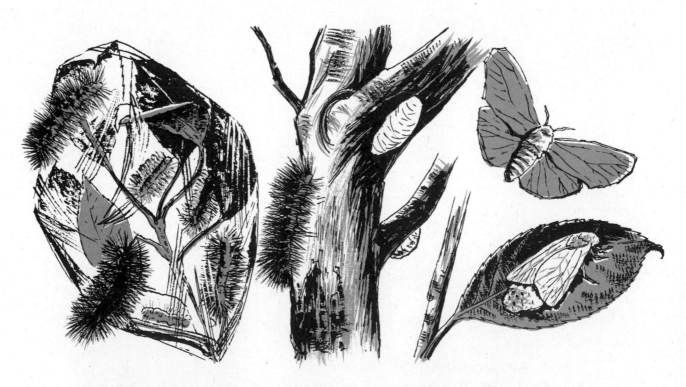

In late summer, these caterpillars live all together in a tent that they spin. Then, in fall, each one spins a silken cocoon around itself. All winter the silk threads hold the cocoon fast to a tree branch. By spring the caterpillar has changed into a moth, which breaks out of the cocoon and flies away. Finally, the female lays on a leaf a mass of eggs which turn into new caterpillars.

WHERE DO THE STARS GO IN DAYTIME?

AT NIGHT when you fall asleep the sky is full of stars. In the morning not one can be seen. The stars seem to disappear when daylight comes, but they don't really go away. There are stars in the sky all day, even though we can't see them. They keep on shining, but the sunlight is much brighter than starlight, and so our eyes see only the brightness of the daytime sky.

WHY IS MILK PASTEURIZED?

MILK that has been pasteurized is milk that has been heated and kept hot, but not quite boiling hot, for half an hour. Heating milk in this special way kills any germs in it that might make us sick. The word "pasteurize" comes from Pasteur, the name of the French scientist who discovered how to keep germs from spoiling food.

WHY DO WE HAVE TO KEEP PUTTING WATER IN THE FISHBOWL?

TWO OR THREE times a week we have to add water to the fishbowl. Where does it all go? We can't see the water disappearing, but it does leave the bowl. One after another, invisible small droplets disappear.

These smallest drops of water are called molecules, and they are always moving around. Even when the water looks perfectly still, the molecules bump and shove against each other. Some of them bounce off into the air. The water is evaporating. Only a few molecules bounce away at a time, but if we forget our fishbowl for many days, all of the water will evaporate.

When we heat water, the molecules bounce faster and farther. They bounce out of a boiling hot pan so fast that the pan is soon dry. Clothes dry faster in warm weather than in cold weather because the water molecules move out into the air more quickly.

WHAT IS A MUMMY?

A MUMMY is a dead animal or human being whose body has been preserved. The skin looks as if it had changed to leather, and it lasts for hundreds or even thousands of years.

Long, long ago in ancient Egypt someone discovered the secret of using oils and spices and chemicals to preserve flesh. Mummy-making became part of the Egyptian religion. The bodies of dead kings and queens were carefully prepared and then stored away in beautiful boxes in secret tombs. Many of the tombs have now been found, and thanks to the person who invented the strange custom of making mummies, we know what the Egyptians looked like so long ago.

In our own Southwest the bodies of ancient people were also preserved, but in a different way. There the climate was so dry that the flesh grew leathery after death without any special treatment. Archeologists have found mummies wrapped in turkey-feather blankets and stored in the closed rooms of houses. They have discovered others buried in the earth where moisture couldn't reach them. Thanks only to the dry air of the Southwest, we know what the ancestors of present-day Indians looked like.

The Egyptians made mummies of cats and baboons as well as people. These animals were so useful that they became sacred. Cats helped hunters to catch waterfowl, the way dogs do today. The baboons were trained to pick fruit from tall trees. Sometimes mummies of beetles, dogs and mice were buried in people's graves just to keep the dead spirits company and to make them feel at home.

DO INDIANS HAVE TO LIVE ON RESERVATIONS?

INDIANS are citizens of the United States. They can leave their reservations when they want to, and they can stay away forever if they choose. But many Indians prefer to live on their reservations where their friends and relatives live. They or their tribes own the land there, and that is where they have their homes.

Here are some famous Indian citizens of the United States:

Allie Reynolds, pitcher for the Yankees (Creek Indian tribe).

Maria and Marjorie Tallchief, ballet dancers (sisters who have Osage ancestors).

John N. Garner and Charles Curtis, Vice-Presidents of the United States (Garner, part Cherokee; Curtis, part Osage and Kaw).

ARE SNOWFLAKES ALL DIFFERENT?

PEOPLE who have looked at many, many snowflakes say they've never seen two alike. Of course, no one has studied all the snow in the world. If you wanted to spend the rest of your life looking, you just *might* find two flakes that are shaped almost alike, but probably they wouldn't be exactly the same.

WHICH ANIMALS ARE THE SMARTEST?

THE SMARTEST kind of animal is now staring at some little black marks which look like this: The smartest kind of animal . . .

You belong to the group of animals that are smartest.

What animals, next to human beings, have the most intelligence? Horse lovers, of course, say horses take the prize. Scientists believe that a chimpanzee has a brain most nearly like ours. Certainly it can learn to do many things. It can figure out how to work the machines that give you candy bars when you put money in the slot.

An elephant, too, can solve problems. If its skin itches in a spot that its trunk can't reach, it will use a stick as a scratcher. Members of an elephant herd can learn to work together as a team, and they help other members who get sick or injured. Dolphins also help each other. Some scientists believe a dolphin is so intelligent it can learn to use human language.

Perhaps you believe that ants are really the smartest creatures. They live together in colonies that resemble big towns. In some colonies there are soldiers who fight off enemies, nursemaids who care for babies, even workers who plant gardens and raise food. But the ants don't *think* when they do all these things. They don't plan activities ahead of time. They work together because they were born with the habit of working together. A built-in pattern guides them. Ants do not solve problems by inventing new ideas. Only men can really invent new ideas.

92

WHAT IS THE BIGGEST ANIMAL?

THE BIGGEST CREATURE in the world is the blue whale. If you could stretch one out across a baseball diamond with its nose on home plate, its tail would almost reach second base. A blue whale weighs as much as 150 tons, and it is very powerful. It can sink a small ship if it chooses to bash in the side with a blow of its tail. Although it lives in the sea, you mustn't call it a fish. Whales are mammals. That is, they have warm blood, and the mothers feed their babies on milk from their bodies. A mother whale lies on her back in the sea while the huge baby suckles.

Is the blue whale the largest of all babies when it is first born? Yes, but there's another way of thinking about size. Suppose you compare a baby to its parents. For instance, most human mothers weigh twenty or twenty-five times as much as their new-born babies. If you think about size in this way, then the baby porcupine is the biggest. A mother porcupine weighs only three times as much as her baby when it is born.

WHERE DOES WOOD GO WHEN IT BURNS UP?

YOU PUT a big stick of wood on the fire, and soon there is nothing left but a small pile of ashes. What happened to the rest of the wood? Where did it go? It went up the chimney.

You can see some of it going up when you see the smoke that burning wood makes. But a fire often burns without much smoke at all. This always happens when the wood gets very hot. If you blow a stream of air onto red-hot wood, it burns very quickly. The air and the hot wood together change into invisible gases. These hot gases are very light. They are so light that they fly away through the chimney. When wood burns up, it really does go up.

WHY DON'T WE FEEL THE WORLD GOING AROUND?

EVERY DAY we take a giant merry-go-round ride. The earth turns around and around. We in the United States are spinning through space right now about seven hundred miles an hour. But we don't feel as if we are moving. Why not?

Even with eyes shut we know that a merry-go-round is moving. We feel it wiggling and joggling as it turns. We hear little creaking noises, too. These are clues that tell us we're in motion.

The earth gives us none of these feeling clues. It whirls smoothly, noiselessly in space. It spins without any joggles or bumps.

With eyes open when we ride on a merry-go-round, we have other clues. People, buildings, trees — we see them one after another as we go past, and we see them over and over.

Of course, the sun and the stars do give us seeing-clues. But it takes twenty-four whole hours before we pass by the same spot twice. So we don't get any sense of motion through our eyes. In fact, we have a feeling that it is the sun and stars, not we, that are moving.

IS A TORNADO THE SAME AS A HURRICANE?

A TORNADO is a great whirling windstorm. The wind goes round and round, in a huge spiral, from earth to a great black cloud in the sky. The wind blows so hard that it can lift the roof off a house. The middle of a tornado is like a giant vacuum sweeper. It can suck up an automobile and carry it away! Tornadoes always blow over land, and as a rule they travel about twenty-five miles before they finally stop whirling. Luckily the path of a tornado isn't very wide — only about a quarter of a mile — and it usually lasts less than an hour.

A hurricane is also a vast whirling storm. But it always starts over the ocean near the equator. It is many, many miles wide, so you can't actually see or feel the circular motion of the wind. Its center doesn't suck things upward the way a tornado does. Instead the center is calm and peaceful, while the storm roars around and around it. As a hurricane travels from south to north day after day, it often moves away from the ocean and passes across land, causing great destruction.

Weathermen are learning more and more about these fierce storms. The more they know, the easier it is to warn people to get ready ahead of time. Perhaps some day weather scientists may even learn how to stop tornadoes and hurricanes before any damage is done.

What makes a wind suddenly begin to blow in circles? Weathermen give this explanation: Ordinary winds blow when cool air moves in to take the place of warm air that is rising. The mixing of cool and warm is irregular and helter-skelter. But sometimes very cool air streams toward a place where the air is much warmer. Instead of many little irregular whirlpools of mixing air, one larger whirlpool forms, and the tornado or hurricane begins.

HOW NEAR IS THE NEAREST STAR?

OUR SUN is really a star, and it is closer to us than any other. But that probably isn't what you mean when you ask the question. So the answer is this: Beyond the sun, the nearest star is more than 25 trillion miles away.

Distances in space are very great. It is a nuisance to figure them in miles, because there are too many zeros. And so astronomers measure distance by light years. A light year is the number of miles that light can travel in a year. Light travels very fast — about 186,000 miles a second. In a year it goes about six trillion miles.

Let's see what that means. When you look at the nearest star you see a twinkling light. The light you see has been traveling for almost four and a half years! If you are in the fourth grade, the light that you see now left that star when you were still in kindergarten. It has been speeding toward the earth, night and day, ever since then.

If that star seems a long way off, think about this: Astronomers have discovered another star so far away that it takes light two billion years to travel from there to the earth!

WHAT IS THE FASTEST ANIMAL?

THE FASTEST INSECT is probably the botfly which darts along at forty or fifty miles an hour.

Many naturalists think that the duck hawk is the fastest bird, although they don't agree on its speed. Once a racing pigeon was accurately timed. It flew at an average speed of 93½ miles an hour for many miles.

Dolphins are fast swimmers. They can keep up with motor boats traveling thirty miles an hour.

The cheetah, most people agree, can go faster than any other four-legged animal. Its record is about seventy-five miles an hour. Hunters have trained cheetahs to pursue and kill swift-running antelopes and deer. And when there's nothing to hunt, a trained cheetah will race an automobile just for fun.

96

IS LIGHTNING DANGEROUS?

YES, LIGHTNING can be dangerous. If you are outdoors when a thunderstorm blows up, you should go into a house where you will be protected from lightning. In the old days people thought they had to shut their windows to keep the lightning out. They thought it could blow in with the wind. But it really can't.

Lightning usually hits things that are sticking up into the air. It often hits trees. So you should never stay under a tree during a thunderstorm. If you can't run home, it is better to sit or lie down in a low, open place, even if you have to get rained on.

An automobile is a safe place, and so is a cave. Lightning often strikes water, so you shouldn't swim during a thunderstorm. Thunder often seems to be the scariest part of a storm. But thunder can't hurt you at all.

Here is an easy way to tell whether lightning is close to you. Look for the flash and start to count the instant you see it. Count until you hear the thunder. One-and-two-and-three-and-four-and-five-and. If you can count to five in this way, before you hear the thunder, the lightning has struck about a mile away from you, and it can't possibly do you any harm. If you can count to ten, it is two miles away. When lightning is really close, you see the flash and hear the thunder at almost the same moment.

WHY IS THE NORTH POLE CALLED A POLE?

THE NORTH POLE is not like a flag pole. A flag pole is a real rod made of wood or metal. The North Pole is one end of an imaginary rod.

You can get an idea of what the North Pole is if you watch a spinning toy top. The top seems to whirl around as if it had a rod through the middle. The earth spins around just the way a top does, as if it had a rod or axle through it from north to south. Every part of the earth turns around this imaginary rod, and the imaginary ends of it are the North and South Poles.

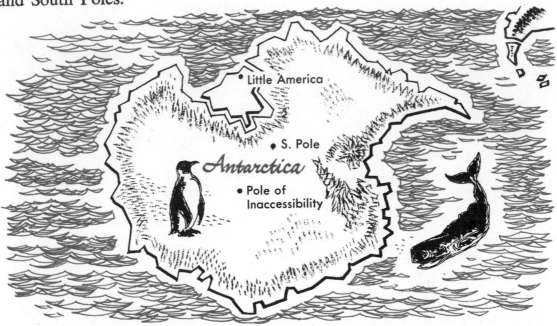

About six hundred miles from the South Pole there is a spot which is harder to reach than any other place in the world. It lies on a high plain, more than two miles above sea level, and the air is so thin that explorers have trouble breathing. Their sleds and tractors can scarcely travel through the soft, fluffy snow. The temperature goes down to 114 degrees below zero. Scientists call this place the *Pole of Inaccessibility*.

HOW LONG DOES IT TAKE TO COUNT TO A MILLION?

THAT DEPENDS on how fast you can count. But suppose that it takes you one minute to count to 100. Now suppose you keep on at that rate for eight hours. If you count for eight hours every day, you will reach one million at the end of 20 days, 6 hours and 40 minutes. Almost three weeks!

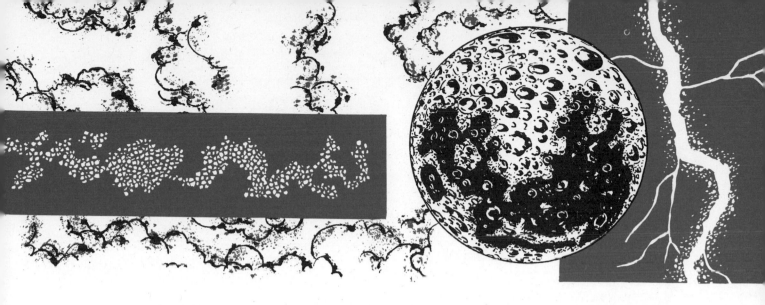

CHAPTER VI

Beginnings

AT CERTAIN PLACES under the hard rock crust of the earth there are pools of hot *liquid* rock. Perhaps radioactivity has heated these places so that the rock is molten. Experts aren't sure about this, but they know that the hot liquid rock moves toward the surface through any cracks or weak places in the solid rock above it. It even dissolves hard rock, making weak places through which to push.

In one way or another it manages to get out onto the surface, and we call it lava. Lava may break free suddenly with a tremendous explosion. Or it may flow out of a big crack. When it does this it looks and acts somewhat like honey.

A volcano is formed when hot lava escapes from the earth.

Some volcanoes shoot "ash" into the air. As this volcanic ash falls back to earth it builds up a cone-shaped mountain around the hole out of which it comes. One day in 1943 a farmer in Mexico saw smoke coming from a three-inch hole that had suddenly appeared in his cornfield. The hole grew and began to spew out volcanic ash. In a week the ash had built up a cone 500 feet high. A few weeks later it was 1000 feet high and still growing. A new volcano had been born.

The ash out of which the volcano grew was not real ash. It was lava

A mountain called Vesuvius in Italy suddenly exploded nearly 2,000 years ago. Deadly gases poured down over the neighboring city of Pompeii and killed almost all the people there. Then volcanic ash settled over everything, burying the city. By digging up Pompeii scientists have learned a great deal about how people looked and lived in the ancient world.

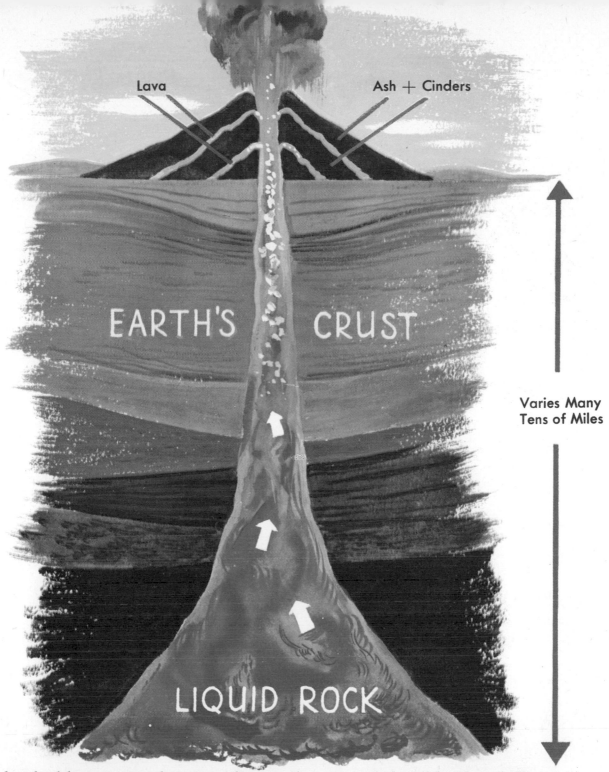

Lava

Ash + Cinders

EARTH'S CRUST

Varies Many
Tens of Miles

LIQUID ROCK

that had been sprayed up into the air where it cooled and hardened. But it only cooled *after* it had grown hotter than it was down inside the earth. Lava grows hotter when it mixes with oxygen. The same thing happens when it touches water. Some volcanoes, erupting under water at the bottom of the ocean, keep building themselves up until they become islands. Hawaii is a group of volcanic islands.

101

HOW DOES A TURTLE GET INTO ITS SHELL?

This box turtle has eaten too much of its favorite food, strawberries. It has grown so fat that it is almost too big for its shell.

TURTLES HATCH from eggs. A baby turtle comes into the world with a shell just the right size for it. As the turtle grows, the shell grows.

If something frightens a turtle, it pulls its head, legs and tail into the shell. Then very few enemies can get at it.

WHERE DOES OUR ENERGY COME FROM?

WE CAN WALK and run, work and play because we have energy. Our energy comes from the sun, but we don't have to be outdoors to get it. It comes to us stored up in foods. The fruits and vegetables we eat received energy from sunlight when they were growing. Our milk and eggs and meat come from animals, but *they* got their energy from plants. So our energy really does come from the sun.

HOW DID THE UNIVERSE GET STARTED?

MANY SCIENTISTS believe that there was always a universe and that there always will be a universe. In other words, it didn't get started. It has always been there. But particular stars and planets and shooting stars have not always been the way they are now. Each of them did have a beginning. Each of them has changed a great deal since that beginning. Old stars are always fading out and shriveling up. Shooting stars are always coming to a sudden end when they bump into some larger body in space. And somewhere in the universe new stars are always being formed.

HOW DO WORMS GET INTO APPLES?

THE SWEETEST APPLE is the one where you'll find the most little tunnels made by the railroad worm. The worm was born inside the apple, which becomes both home and grocery store.

It all begins in the middle of summer when a small fly buzzes around the orchard. She alights on an apple — the sweet kind, if she can find one. Then with a sharp, hollow little tube on her underside she jabs a hole in the fruit. Eggs slide down through the hollow tube into the apple. Before long these eggs hatch. The creatures that come from the eggs do not look like their mother at all. They are tiny white railroad worms. From now until autumn the worms chew tunnels through their food supply. Then, when the apple falls from the tree, they crawl into the ground, and a hard outside skin forms around each one.

The skin will be the worm's winter home. Inside that home an amazing thing happens. The worm changes into a fly. Next summer the fly comes out of the skin, just at the time when apples are growing sweet.

These are the four forms of the worm that eats holes in an apple. Many insects change from one form to another as they grow older. This changing of form is called metamorphosis.

WHAT IS A TADPOLE?

BABY FROGS are called tadpoles or polliwogs, and they don't look like their parents at all. They look more like fish. They even breathe like fish, taking all the oxygen they need from the water. They get this oxygen through gills at the sides of the head. Look at the pictures and you will see how tadpoles grow up and turn into frogs.

Frogs have a special name because they start life in the water and then move out onto land. They are called amphibians, which means "living a double life."

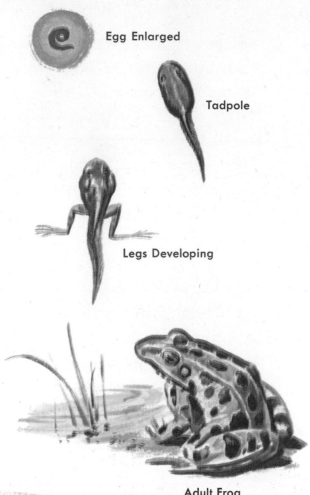

Egg Enlarged

Tadpole

Legs Developing

Adult Frog

Toad

Newt

Salamander

Frogs, toads, newts and salamanders are amphibians.

WHAT SET THE SUN ON FIRE?

How DID the sun begin in the first place? All of space seems to be filled with a very thin gas. This gas is not spread evenly. At places it is thicker than at others. Here and there it is thick enough to contain solid or liquid particles and to look like a cloud. Apparently light from the stars pushes this thin gas around, and it keeps on pushing when it has formed a cloud. The cloud develops into a kind of whirlwind — or a whirling collection of whirlwinds.

Something like that happened about six billion years ago to one huge dust cloud which became our sun. Its particles and gases crowded closer and closer together. They squeezed and crowded together so hard that the pressure began to create heat. Finally the heat turned one of the gases called hydrogen into another gas called helium. This is just what happens when an H-bomb explodes. The sun had become a gigantic H-bomb!

Now there was a tremendous increase in heat and light. Scientists estimate that the sun has enough hydrogen in it to keep going at the present rate for a very, very long time. But at last the sun will have changed so much that a new thing will happen. It will suddenly get even hotter. The heat will be so tremendous that it will burn up everything on earth and boil away the seas.

This flare-up will last only a short time, and then the sun will suddenly shrivel and grow cold and dark.

You don't have to worry about all this. Experts say that the sun's final burst won't happen until about six billion years from now.

HOW DID OIL GET INTO OIL WELLS?

MILLIONS of years ago plants and animals made the oil we get from oil wells today. At that time the places where we find oil were covered by seas. Countless numbers of plants and animals lived in the sea water and fell to the muddy bottom when they died. Layers of mud and sand piled up on the sea floor. Sometimes the layers became thousands of feet thick, and they gradually turned to rock.

The mud that held the decaying plants and animals turned to rock, too. Tiny oily droplets and tiny bubbles of gas were all that remained of the ancient sea life. Very small holes or pores in the rock held these bubbles and droplets. The rock held water in its pores, too. But water and oil don't stay mixed. The oil rises to the top. And gas rises above the oil. So, deep underground, oil and gas and water separated. Through connecting pores in the rock water moved slowly downward. Droplets of oil and bubbles of gas moved slowly upward.

At last the oil and gas reached a layer of rock that had no pores in it. They could move no farther upward, and there they stayed. Sometimes a pool of oil collected in a cavern deep underground. Gas was also trapped and squeezed into the space on top of the oil.

Ages and ages later men drilled wells to get the oil that had collected in the rocks and caverns. When the well hole first reached oil, the pressure of the gas was often so great that it pushed the oil thousands of feet upward. It caused a fountain of oil called a gusher.

106

WHERE DID THE MOON COME FROM?

THE MOON belongs to the sun's family. So we have to find out first where the whole family came from. Many scientists think that the sun began as a kind of lump in a vast cloud of gas and dust. But the sun wasn't the only lump there. It was just the biggest one, and it was in the center. Countless smaller lumps began to collect in the cloud that whirled around the big one in the center. Countless times these lumps bumped into each other and stuck together. Numberless pygmy planets developed. They all circled the sun, keeping the motion of the original whirling cloud in which they formed.

Again and again these undersized planets collided, as millions of them kept wheeling around and around. Like rolling snowballs, a few of them grew quite large. These became full-sized planets.

But some of the pygmies behaved differently from all the rest, and one of them turned out to be our moon. It came close to the planet earth, but it didn't bump. It was moving at such high speed that it managed to fly on past. But then it changed course. The earth's gravity had captured it! From then on the pygmy planet circled the earth. Other pygmies were captured by the gravity of other planets, and they, too became moons. Mars has two of them. Jupiter has twelve.

Some scientists have another idea about our moon. They think it is a big chunk of the earth itself that broke loose long ago.

The surface of our moon is covered with scars which many scientists believe were made when other pygmy planets crashed into it.

A cave man's painting from a European cave.

A cave explorer is called a spelunker. Never go into a cave without an experienced spelunker to tell you how to avoid danger — and how to have a good time.

DID CAVE MEN MAKE CAVES?

PREHISTORIC cave men *found* caves and lived in them; they didn't have to make them. There are natural caves in many places all over the world. In a few places people have dug caves out of soft rock, but these people weren't the original cave men.

Natural caves have been made in several ways. Ocean waves pounded against rocky cliffs along the shore and dug sea caves. Giant gas bubbles inside the hot liquid lava from volcanoes became caves when the lava cooled. But most caves were made by water eating holes in rock underground.

How can water eat rock? First of all it must be rock of a special kind. Limestone is a good kind of rock for caves. Second, the water must contain an acid that eats the stone. Ordinary rain water has acid in it!

Now let's see what happened when limestone caves were being formed. Water seeped down from the surface, found tiny holes and cracks in the rock, and filled them up. Gradually the acid in the water ate away the rock. It actually dissolved the limestone and made the holes larger. This took thousands of years, because the amount of acid in the water was very small. Ever so slowly the holes grew until some of them were enormous. Now there was a cave underground, completely filled with water. Then changes took place in the earth, and all the water drained out. The cave was filled with air.

But the story didn't end here. Rain kept falling on the land above the cave. Water kept seeping down through the rock and dissolving more of it. Drop by drop the water oozed out onto the ceiling of the cave. Now the water evaporated, but it didn't take the dissolved limestone with it into the air. The limestone stayed behind — a tiny particle of hard rock stuck to the ceiling of the cave. More drops of water added more rock, and gradually an icicle-shaped stone grew *downward* from the ceiling. Sometimes fast dripping water built *up* another stone below this on the floor of the cave.

Water, which made the cave in the first place, was now busy filling it with beautiful decorations!

HOW CAN FISH EGGS CHANGE INTO FISH?

THESE MOTHER FISH have laid their eggs in water. Each egg is called a cell. All by itself an egg cell cannot change and grow into a baby fish. The egg cell must be joined by another cell called a sperm. Sperm cells come from the father fish.

As the mother fish lays her eggs, the father swims nearby. He lets a liquid flow from his body over the eggs. This liquid contains the sperm cells. Each tiny sperm cell has a long, thin tail for swimming. Soon the sperm cells and egg cells have joined and become part of each other. The egg is ready to change and grow into a baby fish.

Inside the egg's soft covering wonderful changes happen very fast. At first there is only one blob of cell material. Then the blob divides itself in two. It becomes two cells. These divide. Now there are four. An hour or two later, a great many very little cells have been formed. Now even more wonderful changes begin. The cells group themselves into patterns and layers. Finally these groups of tiny cells turn into eyes, skin, bones, blood — all the parts that make up a fish. In about two weeks the baby is ready to break through the egg cover and swim about by itself.

Other animals begin life in this same way. Cats, dogs, horses, people — all of them have fathers and mothers. All of them come from egg cells that have been joined by sperm cells. But there are differences, too. These babies grow in special sacs inside their mothers. The father places the sperm cells in an opening in the mother's body. Since sperm cells can move, the sperm quickly joins the egg cell, and the wonderful changes begin. Cells divide and group themselves and grow, until at last a new baby is born.

WHERE DO CLOUDS COME FROM?

CLOUDS HIDE the sun and rain begins to fall. Sometimes it keeps falling for hours. Where does all that water come from?

Water to make the clouds comes from the ocean. It comes from lakes and ponds, rivers and brooks. Everywhere water is constantly evaporating — floating in invisible drops up into the air to make clouds. Sooner or later this same water comes back to earth again in rain or snow or hail or sleet. Rain water runs into rivers. Rivers flow into the ocean. So water is always moving in a great cycle — from earth to clouds, then down again. Imagine — the rain on your roof was rain on somebody else's roof before you were born! It fell on the dinosaurs in swampy jungles 70 million years ago. That same bit of water may have made flowers grow in Japan. Maybe it was once part of an Eskimo child's snow house. Perhaps it gave a thirsty Arab a drink. Who knows — some day it may go in a rocket ship to Mars!

HUNDREDS OF BUTTERFLIES, thousands of mosquitoes, millions of beetles and grasshoppers and bees! How can there be so many of them in summer? Where do they all come from? They come from eggs.

A queen bee lays eggs all day every day in summer. Just one queen can lay tens of thousands in a few months. A termite lays several million eggs a year. And one kind of wasp is champion of them all. She lays eggs that produce twins — not just one pair of twins from each egg, but 150 pairs of twins. That makes 300 young wasps from one single egg!

It's lucky for us that only part of these eggs hatch out. If all of them hatched, and if all the little ones grew up, there soon wouldn't be room in the world for people. Birds eat many of the eggs. Other animals eat them, too. Still, plenty of them do produce young which turn into creeping, crawling, flying creatures that people call "bugs."

The correct name for most crawlers and flyers is not "bug" but "insect." A grown-up insect is easy to recognize. It has a head with feelers. It has a middle part where six legs are attached — three on each side. It has an abdomen. No legs are ever attached to the abdomen. Some insects, but not all, have wings. Can you tell which of the creatures in the pictures are insects?

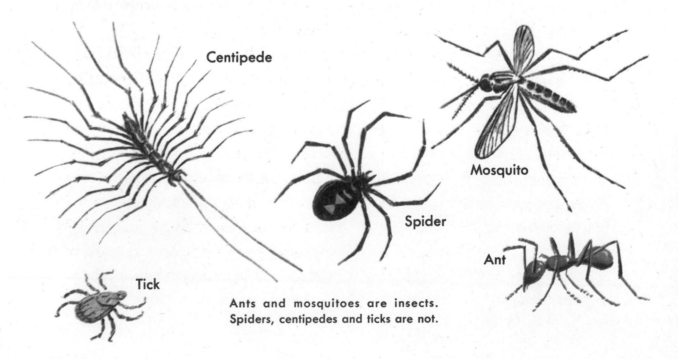

Centipede

Mosquito

Spider

Ant

Tick

Ants and mosquitoes are insects.
Spiders, centipedes and ticks are not.

CHAPTER VII

What Makes Things and Why?

WHAT MAKES WINDOWS GET STEAMY?

IF YOU DRAW a picture on a steamy window, your finger gets wet. Where did the water come from? It came out of the air. There is always water in the air everywhere — tiny droplets of water that you can't see.

All these bits of water bounce around very fast in the warm air of a room. But when they come close to the cold window, something happens to them. They move more slowly. Instead of bouncing off the cold window, some of them stick to the glass. After a while, many, many of them are clinging to the glass. Now there are so many that you can see them. Now you can feel them.

If it is very cold outside, the drops of water freeze on the glass. And that is what makes windows frosty in winter.

WHAT IS QUICKSAND?

THERE ARE MANY stories about quicksand, which is supposed to suck people or horses or cattle down, down until they disappear forever. Quicksand *is* dangerous. A big animal or a person can sink in it and disappear. But quicksand does not actually *suck* anything down. Here is the real story of the mysterious stuff:

Quicksand is ordinary sand *into which water is forced from below*. It forms when a spring pushes water up into a body of sand. Sometimes the spring comes up through sand in the bottom of a river. Or the spring may be far from any stream, and the top layer over the quicksand may even be treacherously dry.

Wherever it is, the spring squirts water up into the sand and keeps it there. It forces the sand to hold more water that it would ordinarily hold. This extra water keeps the particles of sand apart. So when you step on quicksand you are stepping, in a way, on water.

Of course, you can't climb out of water unless you can hold onto something solid — something along the edge of the water or floating on it. In the same way, you need something to help you get out of quicksand.

Even with help you have much harder work getting your feet out of quicksand than out of water. The difference is this: When you lift your foot through water, it leaves no empty space. Water flows immediately into the place where your foot was. But quicksand oozes slowly. You have to give it time to ooze into the empty spot your foot leaves as you pull out. So you have to move slowly to escape from quicksand. If you struggle hard, you will merely push your feet in deeper. This makes it seem as if you are being sucked down.

If you get stuck in quicksand, lie back with your arms out as if you were floating in a swimming pool. Rescuers can get to you if they put boards or a ladder or a tent or even tree branches on top of the quicksand.

WHAT MAKES THE COLORS IN A RAINBOW?

BE A DETECTIVE the next time you see a rainbow. Look for clues that will tell you what causes it. Clue number one: It is daytime. You have never seen a rainbow at night. There aren't any rainbows after dark. They appear only when there is sunlight. Sunlight may be the thing that causes a rainbow's colors.

Clue number two: You don't see a rainbow until there has been rain somewhere. Perhaps you're standing in a dry spot, and the shower has been elsewhere. But rain is involved, as well as sunlight.

Now let's examine the first clue — sunlight. Scientists have noticed what happens to sunlight when it passes through a special kind of glass. They have found that yellowish white sunlight really has all the different colors scrambled together in it.

Is there anything in the sky that can unscramble the colors in sunlight? Can raindrops do the trick? Yes. When sunlight passes through raindrops in just the right way, the light is broken up into many colors and spread out in the sky.

Rainbow colors give a clue to another question: What makes the sky blue? Sunlight's colors can be unscrambled by dust in the air, by gases, by the air itself. These things break light up, and they stop all of the colors except blue. But the blue light bounces away and reaches our eyes. And so the sky looks blue. Of course, only a part of the sun's light is stopped in the sky. The rest of it reaches us still looking yellow-white.

WHAT IS AN ABOMINABLE SNOWMAN?

EXPLORERS in the Himalaya Mountains of Asia tell stories about a strange giant that is supposed to live high up on the cold, snowy peaks. Nobody has ever come close to this mysterious creature, which is called the Abominable Snowman. Some people say they have found its huge footprints. Most scientists doubt that the Snowman is a real animal. But others think it might just possibly be a leftover — a kind of man whose ancestors lived in caves thousands and thousands of years ago.

116

WHAT MAKES AN ECHO?

PEOPLE used to think an echo was made by a kind of fairy who lived in the rocks. When a person shouted something, the echo fairy shouted it right back. Of course, you know that an echo is really the sound of your own voice. You simply hear the sound twice. The sound travels through the air like any other sound. It goes in waves. If you could see the waves, they would look very much like the ripples you make when you drop a pebble into a pool of water. Sound waves travel through the air in every direction.

Suppose you stand in front of a cliff and call out "Hello!" Some of the sound waves hit your ears immediately. Others strike the smooth, hard surface of the cliff, and then they come bouncing back. We say they are reflected. A moment later, these reflected waves reach your ears. And that is how you hear an echo.

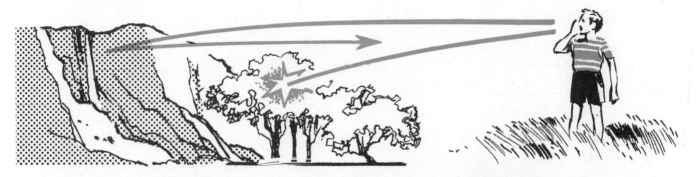

WHY DON'T ALL NOISES HAVE ECHOES?

THERE ARE two reasons why you don't hear an echo every time you make a noise: One reason is that sound waves do not always come bouncing back to you. That is because some things reflect sound better than others. A hard smooth cliff reflects sound better than a hillside covered with trees. In the house curtains and furniture help to keep sound waves from bouncing. Sometimes rooms are lined with a special material that doesn't reflect waves very well. Then we say the rooms are soundproof.

The other reason is that you may be too close to a reflecting surface. The reflected waves bounce back so fast that the sound gets mixed up with the original sound. Instead of hearing a clear echo, you just hear extra noise. That's why big empty rooms are often noisy.

GLACIERS are rivers of ice. They actually flow, and they really are made of ice. Wherever glaciers are found, the average temperature for the whole year is below freezing. This means that ice can last, year after year, even if some of it melts in summer. But where does the ice come from in the first place?

It comes from snow which can change into ice in two different ways. When the sun melts the surface of snow, water seeps down and melts more snowflakes underneath. But the temperature deep in the snow is still below freezing. When the seeping water reaches this super-cold snow, it changes to ice.

But this is not the main way in which snow becomes glacial ice. Snow piles up so deep that the individual snowflakes are pressed close together. When this happens, the tiny snow crystals begin to act according to a special habit they have. The smaller snowflakes join larger ones. The result is new and larger snowflakes or crystals. These crystals then join still larger ones, and so on until solid crystals the size of marbles have been formed. Sometimes in very big glaciers the crystals grow to the size of baseballs.

Glaciers would be mountains of ice getting higher every year if gravity didn't pull on them and make them move downward from the places where they form. Glaciers move slowly, compared to rivers of water, but they do move.

WHERE DOES DEW COME FROM?

DEW COMES OUT of the air. Perhaps the air doesn't seem damp at all, but it does have many little invisible bits of water moving about in it.

At night, after the sun stops warming the earth, the grass cools off quickly. Some of the invisible specks of water in the air come close to the cool grass, and they also get chilled. They move more slowly, and a few of them stick to the grass. One by one the cold specks of water gather until there are so many of them that they join into big drops. Soon you can see them and feel them. These drops of water are dew.

The same thing happens when you fill a glass with ice-cold water on a warm day. The air around the glass is cooled. Drops of moisture collect on the glass. They, too, are dew.

Dew never *falls*. It simply collects on the grass or on anything that is much colder than the air around it. That's why you can walk through the grass in the evening and suddenly find that your feet are quite wet, although the rest of you is dry.

Frost forms on grass or anything else that is very cold. Instead of forming drops, the moisture turns to frosty crystals right out of the air.

You almost never find dew on a cloudy night. Clouds act like a blanket around the earth, and they keep the ground from cooling off. Heat that leaves the earth is turned back by the cloud blanket. Dew does not form because the grass doesn't get cold enough to make the moisture collect in drops. You find dew most often on a clear, cloudless night. So you can see why there is some truth in the old saying: "When the dew is on the grass, rain will never come to pass; when grass is dry at morning light, look for rain before the night."

WHAT MAKES IRON GET RUSTY?

YOU LEAVE your roller skates out in the rain. Next day they have reddish orange spots on them. What has happened? What made them rusty?

Air and rain rusted the iron. Air has oxygen in it, and here is the interesting thing: When oxygen and water and iron come together something happens. The three substances join and produce an entirely new one — rust. We say that air, water and iron have combined and that a chemical change has taken place.

Iron things don't get rusty if they are covered by something that keeps out oxygen and water. Grease or oil will do. Oil forms a thin coat that protects your skates. Paint protects iron fences, bridges and ships.

Silver turns black for almost the same reason that iron gets rusty. Gases in the air or chemicals in food combine with the silver and make a new substance that we call tarnish. Tarnish sticks so tight that we use silver polish to clean it off.

WHY DOES IT RAIN?

RAIN always comes from clouds. But clouds don't always bring rain. Why?

Clouds are made of water — tiny drops of water clinging to little particles of dust. As long as the cloud is warm, these droplets bounce and toss around freely. The first thing that a rain cloud must have is lots of these moisture droplets.

Now suppose that the cloud begins to cool off. The little water-and-dust drops move more and more slowly. They huddle together. Small drops turn into bigger ones. At last they are so big and heavy that they have to fall. And that's what we call rain.

Is snow just frozen rain? No, it is quite different. Frozen raindrops are roundish, and they are called hail and sleet. Snowflakes have beautiful lacy shapes. Each one is a crystal of ice. Each one was formed separately from bits of moisture floating in a storm cloud. Just how and why snow forms into six-pointed crystals the experts can't tell us yet.

Old Faithful is the name of a famous geyser in Yellowstone National Park. It spouts on an average of once every sixty-five minutes.

WHAT MAKES GEYSERS?

A GEYSER is a special kind of spring. Water squirts out of it in jerks, instead of coming in a steady flow, and geyser water is boiling hot.

Hot springs can exist where hot liquid rock is trapped inside solid rock, deep underground. But two special things are needed before a hot spring can become a geyser: (1) underground cavities in which water can collect; and (2) a *narrow* tube leading from the cavities up to the surface.

Here is how a geyser works. Water collects in the cavities. Heat from the liquid rock far below reaches this water and makes it boiling hot. But it can't behave the way ordinary boiling water behaves in a pan on the stove. In the pan, boiling hot water turns to steam; the steam rises from the bottom, and flies off into the air. But the hot water in the geyser cavity can't escape so easily. Remember, there is only a long narrow tube leading to the air outside. The cold water in it acts somewhat like a huge cork in a bottle. The steam can't escape because of the cork. The temperature of the water goes up and up. Still it can't let off steam. Gradually tremendous pressure builds up way down inside the cavity.

Then at last something has to give. Steam presses so hard that water rises through the narrow neck of the geyser and spills over. With this water gone, more water down below turns to steam like a flash. It, too, is pushed out.

Faster and faster, water changes to steam. More and more water is forced up the narrow tube. It rises in a solid column, higher and higher into the air. Then everything stops as suddenly as it began. The cavities down below are empty. They must fill up before the geyser spouts again.

WHY IS IT HOTTER IN SUMMER THAN IN WINTER?

SUMMER AND WINTER, it is the sunshine that warms us. Rays of sunshine pour onto the earth. They warm the roofs of houses and stones in the field. They heat water in ponds and they heat us. When a place on the earth gets a lot of sunshine it is very warm. When that place gets less sunshine it is cooler.

In summer a lot of sunshine pours onto North America. It heats the earth and water, the houses and the fields for many hours each day. And so the weather is hot. In winter earth and water get less of the warming sunshine. And so winter is cold in most of North America.

That is what happens. Look at the pictures and you will see *how* it happens.

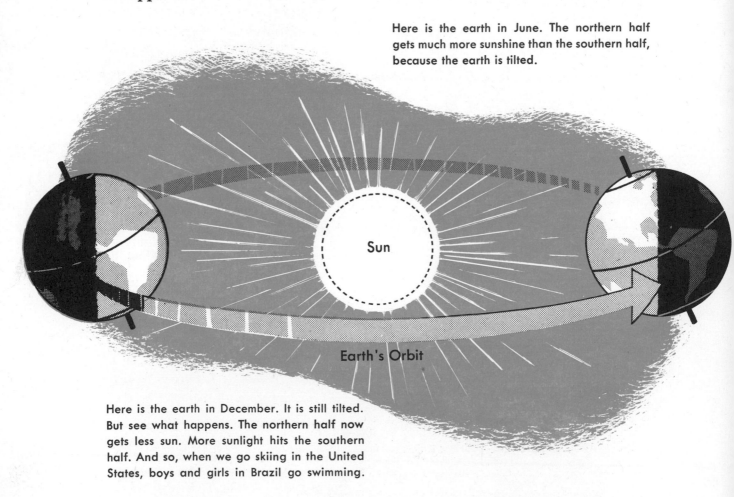

Here is the earth in June. The northern half gets much more sunshine than the southern half, because the earth is tilted.

Sun

Earth's Orbit

Here is the earth in December. It is still tilted. But see what happens. The northern half now gets less sun. More sunlight hits the southern half. And so, when we go skiing in the United States, boys and girls in Brazil go swimming.

122

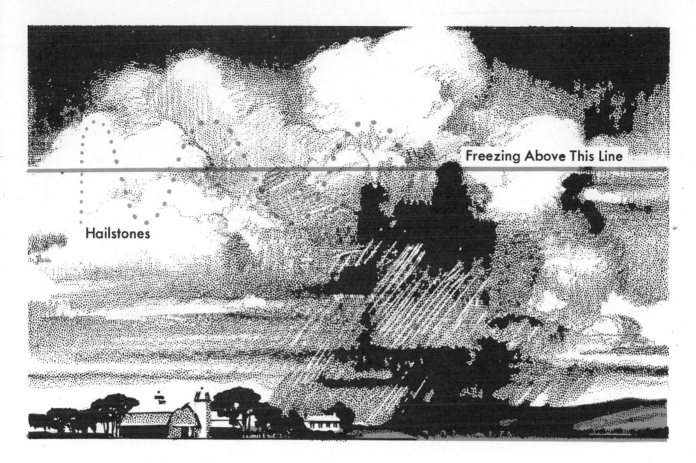

Freezing Above This Line

Hailstones

WHAT MAKES HAIL?

LOOK AT THIS picture of a storm cloud. Great winds are blowing in it, tossing raindrops about. Higher, higher, the winds fling some of the raindrops up where the air is freezing cold. The raindrops turn to ice and start to fall. When they reach the warm part of the cloud, the ice-drops pick up little coats of moisture. But then the wind catches them again. Up they go, carrying along a little water that has stuck to them. The coats of moisture freeze. Down come the ice-drops. Then up they go, over and over, adding more coats and freezing them, until at last the wind lets them fall. A hailstorm suddenly hits us.

Hailstones are often as big as marbles, sometimes as big as tennis balls. The biggest one on record fell in Nebraska. It was about the size of a softball! The man who found it wanted everyone to know that he wasn't telling a tall tale. So he quickly measured his hailstone in front of a town official and signed a paper swearing that it weighed a pound and a half and was seventeen inches around.

TAKE A STICK in your hands and bend it. If you let go, the stick goes back toward its original shape. It is elastic. But if you bend it enough, it will break, and you will feel a tingling in your hands. Your hand tingles because the breaking of the wood made the two parts of the stick vibrate very fast. The vibration that causes the tingling in your hands is like the quake of an earthquake!

When someone tells you that there has been an earthquake, you can be fairly sure of one thing: Someplace the hard rock crust of the earth has bent more than it can stand. The rock snapped, and the earth vibrated.

Parts of the earth's crust are always moving. Proof of this can be seen in many places. One is on the coast of Italy. There the ancient Romans long ago built a big building near the sea. The coast gradually sank until the building was covered by water. Then, hundreds of years later, it rose out of the water. Now it is sinking again.

Sometimes rock snaps, deep down below the surface of the earth where the break can't be seen. Scientists using delicate instruments can study these hidden earthquakes as well as others that result from the shifting of rock that has been under strain. The same instruments also help scientists study a different kind of earthquake that is caused by the explosion of a volcano — or an A-bomb or an H-bomb.

Sometimes when rock snaps in an earthquake, part of it moves up or down. Other times the rock actually rips. The two parts slide sideways past each other.

WHAT IS A FOSSIL?

DID YOU ever break a stone in two and find something inside that looks like a picture of a fern or a clam or a fish or a bug? We call these things fossils, and they are more than pictures. They are the real shapes of real plants and animals that lived on earth long, long ago.

How could a plant or animal get inside a hard piece of rock? This is the story of one fossil fish: Millions of years ago it died and fell into the mud at the bottom of a lake. A river brought more mud down from the mountains and dumped it on top of the fish. At last the river had piled up many layers of mud and sand, one on top of the other. By now the fish's body was no longer the same as it had been. Minerals from the water had taken the place of flesh and bone. But nothing disturbed the spot where it lay, and so its shape stayed there, molded in the mud.

After a long time, the mud began to harden. It turned to stone. Then came great changes in the earth's surface. The ground under the lake heaved and moved upward. The rock with our fish in it was pushed up, high and dry. And there it stayed till we found it.

The rocks hold many kinds of fossils. Besides plants and animals themselves, you can sometimes find burrows where animals lived. The one in the picture is called a "devil's corkscrew," and it was probably the home of a prehistoric beaver. Fossil worm tracks and dinosaur footprints are often found. (After G. G. Simpson.)

These fossil footprints had scientists fooled for almost a hundred years. They look as if they had been made by an animal that crossed its feet with every step it took! Finally someone figured out that the animal had a little toe that resembled a thumb. It was probably a relative of the dinosaurs. (After Peabody.)

HOW DOES YEAST MAKE BREAD RISE?

A PACKAGE of yeast is really a package of little plants. Each yeast plant is so small that you can't see it separately, but when you get a lot of them together in a package you can see lumps of them. One yeast plant by itself under a strong magnifying glass looks like a knobbly potato. The knobs are buds. When a bud grows big enough it breaks off and grows into a separate new plant with buds of its own.

Yeast plants grow in warm, moist bread dough. As they grow they give off a gas called carbon dioxide. This is the same gas that bubbles up and makes soda pop fizz. The gas bubbles up through bread dough, too. It puffs the dough out with hundreds and hundreds of little balloon-shaped bubbles. As the bread bakes in the oven the dough stiffens around the bubbles. And so the holes in the bread are really little dough balloons.

WHAT MAKES THE WAVES IN THE OCEAN?

YOU CAN MAKE little waves by blowing hard into a bowl of water. Ocean waves are just the same, only bigger, and the blowing of the wind causes them. Perhaps you have seen waves on a perfectly still day. These waves started far away. Somewhere over the ocean wind pushed against the water and set it into motion. Ripples formed and grew into bigger ripples and finally into waves. The power of wind on water is very great. Waves can travel five thousand miles and more beyond the place where a wind starts them. Some waves are also formed when the tides go in and out.

Sometimes an earthquake or a volcano at the bottom of the sea causes waves. Enormous waves caused by earthquakes are called tidal waves.

SALT comes from rocks. It has to be loosened from solid rock and washed down to the ocean. Heat and cold, freezing and thawing, make cracks in the rocks, and rain washes the salt out.

Every year rivers carry tons and tons of salt, dissolved in water, down to the sea. And yet oceans do not get any saltier. Scientists believe that the water is just about the same now as it was two billion years ago. They aren't quite sure how this can be so. Perhaps all the plants and animals that live in the ocean use up some of the salt.

IS THE OCEAN REALLY BLUE?

A GLASS of ocean water looks clear and colorless, like a glass of drinking water. But if you stand on the deck of a ship and look about you, the water is sometimes blue and sometimes green. What makes the difference? Sunlight makes the difference. Sunlight has no particular color itself, but it is a combination of all the colors of the rainbow. When sunlight falls on the ocean where the water is deep and clear, only the blue color is reflected back to your eyes.

What has happened when ocean water looks green? Billions of tiny plants and animals have grown in the water. They reflect green light. And so the sea looks green.

LIGHTNING is really electricity — lots of electricity that jumps through the air in huge sparks.

You can make little jumping sparks of electricity if you rub a cat's fur or comb your hair with a hard rubber comb. Probably the giant sparks of lightning are caused in somewhat the same way.

Lightning sparks start in the clouds. Great winds blow through a rain cloud and whip the raindrops around and tear some of them apart. Tremendous action goes on, and this action electrifies the cloud. Weathermen don't know exactly how it happens, but great charges of electricity build up. Suddenly there comes a flash. The lightning jumps from one part of the cloud to another. Or it leaps between the cloud and the earth.

Lightning usually seems like one enormous quivering spark, but it is really several sparks. It travels in a zigzag path, and that is what gives it a jagged look.

If you could stretch electric cords from the ground to the clouds, there wouldn't be any lightning. The electricity would run through the cords into the earth. Of course, we can't plug cords into the clouds. But people often do have metal lightning rods that stick up above houses and barns. The electricity jumps from the cloud to the rod. Instead of hitting the building, it runs into the earth.

THUNDER SOUNDS as if huge things were crashing together in the sky. That is just what happens. Huge quantities of air *do* crash together during a thunderstorm. Lightning is the cause of the crashing.

As lightning jumps across the sky, it heats the air. The air grows hot so suddenly that it gives a terrific push outward. This leaves an almost empty space along the lightning's path. A moment later cold air rushes in to fill the space. Air from one side bumps into air from every other side. There is so much bumping that it makes a tremendous noise.

Thunder rolls and surges and rumbles. That is because the lightning jumps in uneven flashes. Sometimes thunder has extra rumbles. These are echoes that come from hills and valleys and from the clouds themselves.

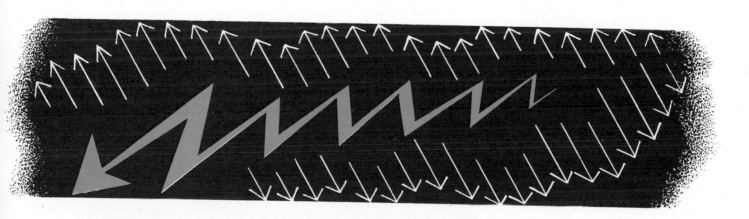

WHY DO WE SEE THE LIGHTNING BEFORE WE HEAR THUNDER?

THE LIGHT and sound of a thunderstorm have to travel to our eyes and ears. Light travels very fast. It goes about 186,000 miles in just one second. That is seven times the distance around the world in the time it takes you to say your name. But sound travels more slowly. In one second it goes only about a fifth of a mile. That is about as long as four football fields laid end to end. Since light travels faster than sound, we usually see lightning before we hear thunder. Only if the lightning strikes very close do we sense both at almost the same instant.

WHAT MAKES PEOPLE HAVE DIFFERENT COLORED SKINS?

YOUR COLOR comes from chemicals in your skin. All people have these same chemicals, but not in the same amounts. Dark-skinned people have large amounts. Pinkish-white skin means that less of the color substance is present.

Scientists who study human beings do not yet know why some of us have more of the color chemicals and some have less. They *have* discovered that outside color does not make people different inside. For example, they have proved by tests that color has absolutely nothing to do with brains. Smart boys and girls are found equally among all peoples, no matter how much or how little of the color chemicals they have in their skins.

WHAT ARE NOISES MADE OF?

IT'S EASY ENOUGH to hear noises, but you can actually *see* how a noise is made if you have a toy drum. Put a few bread crumbs on the drum. Then hit it gently. You hear a soft noise. And you can see the crumbs dancing a little. Now hit the drum harder. You hear a louder sound. The crumbs bounce higher. The noise and the bouncing were made by the same thing. They were made by the top of the drum, which began to wiggle up and down very fast when you hit it. We say the drum vibrated. A gentle hit made it vibrate a little. A hard thump made it vibrate a lot.

How did your ears know that the drum was vibrating? The answer is easy if you remember that there is air all around both you and the drum. When the drum top vibrated, it pushed up on the air and made it move. The drum started a lot of little moving waves in the air. We call them sound waves. And they traveled all the way from the drum to your ears.

Each of your ears has a drum in it, too. An eardrum is a tiny piece of skin stretched tight across an opening inside your head. Of course, an eardrum can vibrate. When sound waves hit your eardrum they made it vibrate. Your vibrating eardrum tells you that the toy drum made a noise.

CHAPTER VIII

Friends and Enemies

ARE INSECTS EVER GOOD FOR ANYTHING?

MANY INSECTS do useful things. Bees make honey. They also help pears and peaches and apples and other fruits to grow. When fruit trees are blossoming, bees carry a yellow powder called pollen from the flowers in one tree to the flowers in another. The bees spread the pollen accidentally while they are looking for nectar, but unless the pollen is spread the trees won't bear fruit. Some butterflies and moths also carry pollen from flower to flower.

A little insect called the lac gives us a red dye. Also shellac can be made from the hard crust or *shell* with which the *lac* insect covers itself.

A certain kind of beetle will destroy goat weed which grows very fast and makes cattle sick. At one time goat weed had spread over many large ranches in the West and made them almost useless. Ranchers solved the problem by bringing in millions of these beetles to eat the weed.

The beetle called the ladybird eats the eggs and young of harmful insects. So does the praying mantis.

One kind of wasp kills the worm that eats ears of corn. The horse guard wasp catches flies that bite horses. The wasp zooms along, snatches a fly in mid-air and stings it to death. Then she carries it off to her nest for the young wasps to eat.

WHAT MAKES BEES AND WASPS STING?

A BEE STINGS in order to protect its hive. Robber bees sometimes try to raid hives and steal honey. So do mice. When this happens there is a good chance that the raiders will be killed by stings. One bee's venom can poison a mouse many times its size.

Bees also sting people who make quick, threatening gestures. And there seem to be other things that irritate bees and set them to stinging. One is the odor of strong perfume. Another is the way you smell when you need a bath!

Many wasps, too, attack enemies with their stings. But there is one kind of wasp that has another use for a stinger. The female makes it provide food for her young. First she finds a caterpillar. Then she gives it an injection of her stinging fluid. This paralyzes the caterpillar. The wasp now lays eggs in the helpless creature. The baby wasps that hatch out of the eggs feed on the caterpillar until they are big enough to go off and take care of themselves.

ARE SHARKS DANGEROUS?

SOME KINDS of sharks are dangerous. They will attack human beings in the water. Skin-divers have to watch out for them. And swimmers should stay on the beach when sharks are reported.

Some sharks are very small. They snap at an ocean fisherman's bait hungrily. They are pests because they aren't good to eat.

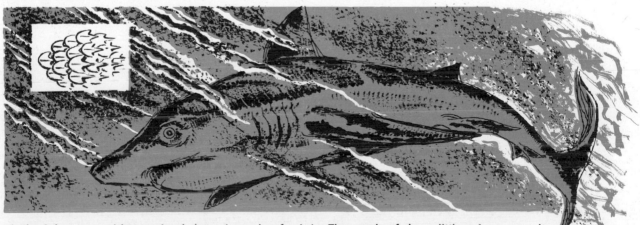

A shark has no real bones. Its skeleton is made of gristle. Thousands of sharp little spines cover its body. The spines are really small teeth! The shark is the only creature that has these skin-teeth.

WHY DO ZEBRAS HAVE STRIPES?

THE STRIPES that seem so conspicuous to us probably help zebras to be overlooked by lions and other animals that like zebra meat. Zebras often stand in very tall grass where it is hard to tell the difference between their stripes and the shadows of the grass blades.

Other creatures have other remarkable ways of hiding from enemies. One kind of grasshopper looks like a leaf — an unappetizing leaf that has already been chewed on by beetles.

A common garden insect called a walking stick has a body that is easily mistaken for a brown twig. A relative of this walking stick looks like a brier twig, bristling with red thorns.

One kind of katydid is dotted with imitation dewdrops that make it hard to see, and there is a certain kind of butterfly you can easily overlook. Its wings look just like dead leaves with patches of mold growing on them.

There are at least two kinds of furry animal that have partners helping them to hide. These partners are tiny plants called algae. They grow on the fur of the animals, and they are green. The green algae make the animals hard to see among the leaves of the trees in the jungles where they live.

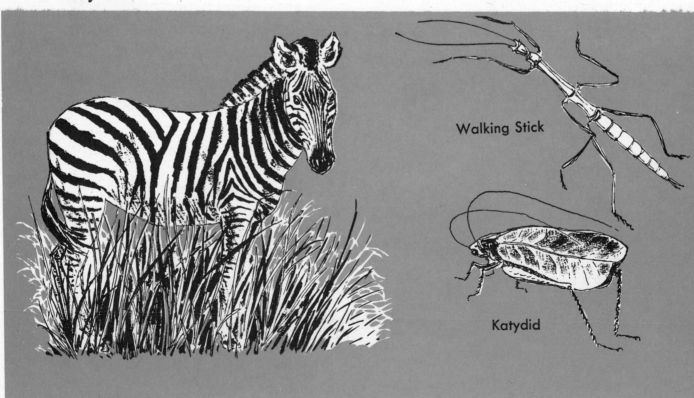

Walking Stick

Katydid

A SKUNK sends an oily spray into the air. The oil has such an unpleasant odor that attackers keep their distance.

A skunk's body manufactures the oil which is stored in little sacs near its tail. When a spotted skunk is frightened, up go its hind quarters. Its body balances on the front feet, and the oil squirts out in a fine spray. The spray won't hurt you, unless it gets directly into your eyes, but it will ruin your clothes. The odor is so hard to remove that most people don't even try.

Skunk oil is very unpleasant to most people, but skunks themselves are friendly little animals. When their oil sacs have been removed, skunks make very good pets.

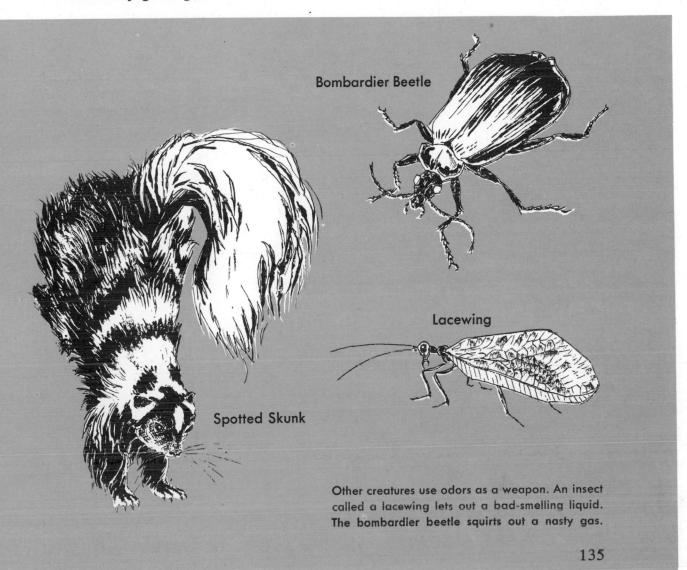

Bombardier Beetle

Lacewing

Spotted Skunk

Other creatures use odors as a weapon. An insect called a lacewing lets out a bad-smelling liquid. The bombardier beetle squirts out a nasty gas.

CAN A PORCUPINE THROW ITS QUILLS?

No, A PORCUPINE cannot shoot out its quills at other animals or human beings. But don't go too close to a porcupine. It may switch you with its tail. The tail, like the body, is covered with quills that stick when they touch anything soft.

Each quill has a sharp point. It can easily go into the mouth or tongue of a foolish bear or mountain lion. Once the quill is in, it clings with a sharp barb, like the barb on a fishhook. Often the quill keeps working its way deeper and deeper into the flesh. Although it is no bigger than a toothpick, it can kill a huge bear. A bear can't use pliers as you can to pull the quill out.

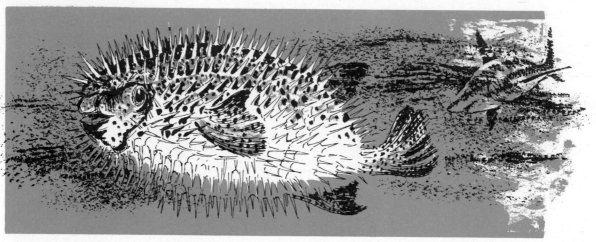

This fish is called a porcupine fish because it has sharp spines that look like quills. If an enemy comes near, it puffs itself up into a ball with its spines sticking out in every direction. Very few bigger fish manage to eat it, but sometimes a shark swallows it whole and that's a bad day for the shark. The porcupine fish has knifelike teeth, and it can gnaw its way out of the shark!

DO ALLIGATORS AND CROCODILES EAT PEOPLE?

IF AN ALLIGATOR is frightened, it will sometimes attack people, but it is not really a man-eater. American crocodiles usually leave people alone. The crocodiles that live in Africa and Asia eat anything they can catch, and they are very dangerous to man.

Sometimes these big-mouthed creatures get eaten themselves. A naturalist once found a huge snake that had swallowed a five-foot alligator!

136

WHAT IS AN ANT COW?

"ANT COW" is really just a nickname for an insect called an aphid. But ants do get food from aphids in somewhat the way people get milk from cows. An ant strokes an aphid with its feelers, and the aphid squirts out a drop of sweet liquid called honeydew which the ant likes to eat.

ARE SNAKES ANY GOOD?

MOST SNAKES are useful because they live on animals like mice and rats that eat up the farmers' crops. But some snakes are very dangerous. They can poison you if they strike you with their fangs. When you find a snake the best rule to follow is this: Don't kill it; don't play with it; don't even try to go near it until someone who really knows about snakes tells you it is safe. Some of the snakes that are safe, like the garter snake, can be fun to keep as pets.

WHAT MAKES A SNOWSHOE RABBIT TURN WHITE IN WINTER?

IN SUMMER a snowshoe rabbit wears a brown coat. But when the nights grow longer and the days shorter, the color of the fur changes. White hairs appear among the brown ones. By winter the rabbit is entirely white. In spring the fur gradually becomes all brown again. What causes these changes?

In order to find out, scientists did an experiment. While the summer days were still long, they began blindfolding a rabbit a little while before darkness fell. Each day they put the blindfold on a little earlier. The rabbit saw a little less light each day, exactly as he would when autumn came. The days only *seemed* shorter, but sure enough, the color of the rabbit's coat changed. It grew white before winter!

This experiment solves only part of the mystery. How can a change in the light the rabbit sees act as a signal for its color to change? And what goes on in the rabbit's body when its fur turns white? More detective work must be done before we can know the answers.

A snowshoe rabbit's color helps it to hide from enemies. The white fur is almost invisible against the snow in the cold country where it lives. Its brown summer coat blends with the rocks and earth there.

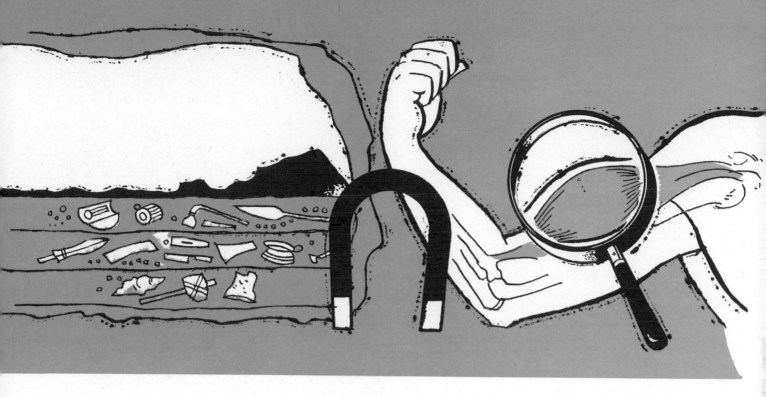

CHAPTER IX

How Do We Know?

HOW DO WE KNOW ABOUT CAVE MEN?

PEOPLE who lived thousands of years ago were untidy. They left garbage, broken tools, and all kinds of trash wherever they camped. When they finished gnawing on a bone, they just tossed it away. Those who lived in caves dropped a great deal of stuff on the floor. They also left ashes from their fires.

Scientists have dug into the floors of some caves and have found layer after layer of trash and ashes. Only human beings could have created this mess. Bears and other animals don't build fires or make arrowheads, chipping off little flakes of flint. Bears don't drop beads and broken pottery around.

By studying the trash heaps, a scientist can learn a great deal about what the cave men ate, the clothes they wore, the tools and weapons they used. It is even possible to examine a skeleton buried in the trash and then figure out what cave men looked like.

In a few European caves ancient artists painted beautiful pictures on rock walls far underground. They used twigs or bits of moss for brushes. They mixed colored clay and vegetable dyes into meat grease for their paints. With only smoky torches for light, these first artists drew wonderful hunting scenes and painted the portraits of animals that have now disappeared from the earth. Only one or two of the pictures show people, but they tell us a great deal about the cave men just the same. These were not stupid creatures who went around hitting each other on the head with clubs. Instead, they were clever inventors and talented artists. They had a sense of humor, too, for they even drew a few cartoons.

The newest trash is naturally on top in the cave floor. Below that each layer is older than the layer above it. Scientists can sometimes tell exactly how old a layer is by studying bits of wood and pottery in it. By digging in ancient trash they can write the story of people who hadn't learned to write!

140

HOW DO WE KNOW THAT PLANTS GROW ON MARS?

OF COURSE, nobody has ever eaten a carrot from Mars, and we don't even know whether Martian vegetables look like ours. But scientists feel sure that plants do grow there.

Mars is quite a lot like the earth. The two are sometimes called "twin planets." Looking through very strong telescopes, men have seen patches of green on Mars. These patches turn brown when autumn comes on Mars, just as leaves turn brown on earth. The following spring, green appears again. It seems likely that only plant life would change color in this way.

HOW DOES THE WEATHERMAN KNOW WHEN IT IS GOING TO RAIN?

ALL BY HIMSELF one weatherman can't tell for sure when it is going to rain. He must have information from other weathermen. He also needs instruments that tell him how much moisture is in the air, how fast the wind is blowing, what the temperature is, and many other things.

Every day more than four hundred watchers in the United States look at their instruments and send telegrams to the Weather Bureau in Washington, telling what the instruments say. This information is passed along to weathermen who use it to figure out if we're going to have rain.

Even with a great deal of information, the weatherman is sometimes wrong about rain. He makes mistakes because scientists still don't know all there is to know about weather and what makes it the way it is.

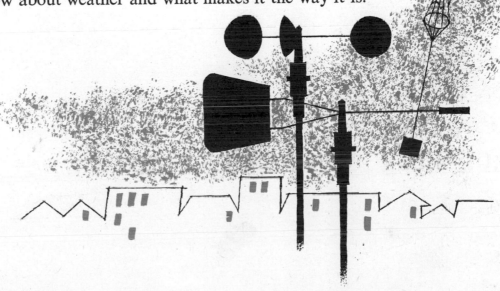

HOW DO WE KNOW WHAT IT'S LIKE INSIDE THE EARTH?

SUPPOSE you could dig a hole four thousand miles deep, straight to the center of the earth. What would you find on the way? Although the deepest oil well only goes down about four miles, scientists have put together many kinds of information, and this is how they think the earth is made from the surface to the center:

First comes a crust of ordinary rock. This is twenty or thirty miles thick in most places. Under the Pacific Ocean it is only a few miles thick.

Next comes a layer of heavier rock about 1,800 miles thick.

Inside this layer is the earth's core. The core seems to be a sort of liquid metal, very hot and much heavier than any metals you have ever seen.

Information about the earth's inside comes from an instrument that was invented for another purpose. This instrument is the seismograph which makes a little wavy line on special paper every time it is joggled by an earthquake. Scientists study these wavy lines to find out when and where the earth is quaking. They have also discovered that the lines can help reveal what *kind* of material the shocks of the earthquake passed through on their way from the quake to the seismograph.

Will we ever have a look at the earth's core itself? Probably not. But some day we will certainly know more about it and what it is made of.

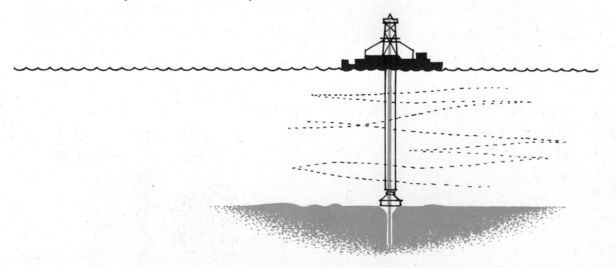

Scientists hope to get a sample of the rock between the earth's crust and core. They plan to drill a deep hole in the floor of the ocean using machinery like this.

HOW DO WE KNOW HOW FAR IT IS TO THE MOON?

LONG, LONG AGO men watched the sky and tried to figure out ways of measuring the things they saw there. How far was it to the moon, for example? These ancient sky watchers were good at mathematics. They did some rather complicated figuring, and they decided that the moon was about 240,000 miles away.

Today sky watchers have a way of testing the figures for us. They do it with radar. They broadcast radio waves which travel to the moon and then bounce back to earth. The radar measuring instruments tell how many seconds it takes the waves to make the round trip. Divide this by two and we know how many seconds it takes the waves just to go to the moon. Since we know how fast radio waves travel, we have only to do some multiplying. We multiply the speed of the waves by the number of seconds it takes for them to reach the moon. The answer is — about 240,000 miles. That's how far you will have to travel when you go by rocket to the moon.

HOW DO WE KNOW WHAT'S GOOD FOR US TO EAT?

LONG AGO a French explorer named Cartier spent a winter on a ship that was frozen tight in the ice of the St. Lawrence River. He had plenty of food aboard, but many of his men grew sick. An Indian chief told Cartier the sailors would be cured if they drank a kind of tea made from the needles of a certain evergreen tree. As if by magic, the tea brought the men back to health. Later, English sailors on long voyages had the same disease. They discovered that the juice of limes would cure it. Both the limes and the evergreen contain a vitamin which is found in fresh foods. The sailors got sick because they had no fresh fruit or vegetables.

Like the sailors, people all over the world have learned by trial and error which foods they must have in order to keep alive. But nowadays food scientists do better than that. They study people and animals. They experiment with foods and chemicals. Gradually they are finding out what the needs of our bodies are and which foods best fill these needs.

WHAT WAS THE FIRST LANGUAGE THAT PEOPLE SPOKE?

NOBODY KNOWS what the first language was. But scientists feel quite sure that nobody speaks it today, because all languages change and keep on changing as long as people use them. One language may change in different ways in different places and grow into several separate languages.

People are always inventing new words. For example, *radium* was made up as a name for a new radioactive substance when scientists discovered it less than sixty years ago.

People forget words, too. For instance, farmers who lived where the winters were snowy usually had *pungs* a hundred years ago. But do you know what a *pung* is?

Words even change in one family. Children don't always use words exactly the way their parents do. They make small changes in the sounds or in the meaning. In time a lot of these little changes add up and make big changes. If we could meet the people who spoke English five hundred years ago, we probably couldn't understand much of anything they said.

English itself is a mixture of several languages. Scientists believe that these languages and many others all grew out of the same ancestor language which they call Indo-European. Nobody speaks Indo-European now, but some of its descendants, besides English, are German, Latin, French, Greek, Russian and many of the different tongues spoken in India.

This is a pung — a kind of sled pulled by horses. Perhaps a hundred years from now your great-great-grandchildren will wonder what the word *bicycle* means.

HOW CAN DUCKS SWIM
WITHOUT HAVING LESSONS?

A BABY DUCK knows how to swim as soon as it hatches from the egg. It doesn't wait to be shown how. It just gets in the water and paddles away. Even if a chicken sits on a duck egg and hatches it, the baby swims like a duck, without lessons. This ready-made knowledge is sometimes called instinct. But how was it made? What causes it? This is still a great mystery. Scientists do not yet know the answer.

All animals have built-in knowledge. Sometimes they do such amazing things that it is hard to believe they don't figure out plans in their minds the way people do. For example, this tree frog builds a little private swimming pool for her babies. First she steals wax from honeybees. Then she uses the wax to make a waterproof lining for a hollow place in a tree-branch where she lays her eggs. Rain fills the hollow. When tadpoles hatch from the eggs they have a hidden pool where they grow up safely.

WHY DID DINOSAURS DISAPPEAR
FROM THE EARTH?

WHAT HAPPENED to the dinosaurs? Why did they all die? This is a puzzle that hasn't been solved. Many scientists believe that the huge creatures disappeared because the climate changed. The warm swampy lands where they lived grew dry and chilly. They couldn't find enough to eat because water plants began to disappear. They grew weak from hunger, and when cold weather came they suffered even more because they were so big they couldn't crawl into caves or holes for shelter. Gradually the dinosaurs all starved to death or died of the cold.

Probably no one will ever find out exactly what happened. But scientists agree on one main idea: The world around the dinosaurs changed. The animals themselves didn't. They couldn't make themselves change to fit their new world. And so they died out.

MANY STRANGE animals used to live in the world. Long, long ago there were huge flying monsters with leathery wings but no feathers. At another time horses were about the size of dogs. Animals resembling elephants had long woolly hair. These and thousands of other ancient animals have all disappeared. How do we know that they ever lived?

Luckily some of them have been preserved in ice. Woolly elephant-like mammoths got frozen and covered with earth in Alaska and Siberia thousands of years ago. The cold kept them perfectly, and from time to time people still find them and dig them out of their natural deep-freeze.

In California something different happened. Many ancient animals fell into a lake of black, sticky tar. The tar was antiseptic, and so the animals' bodies were preserved.

In other places sand or mud covered animals when they died. Their bodies decayed but their bones didn't. Gradually the sand or mud turned to stone. Now, millions of years later, scientists can study the bones preserved in stone. By good detective work they can figure out from the skeletons what the whole bodies must have looked like, thousands or millions of years ago.

Dinosaur National Monument is a place where a great many dinosaurs lived and died about 140 million years ago. Scientists have dug up lots of bones there, and they have cut away one side of a hill, leaving other bones in place, so that visitors can see what the remains of a prehistoric animal look like when it is being discovered.

CHAPTER X

Mysteries

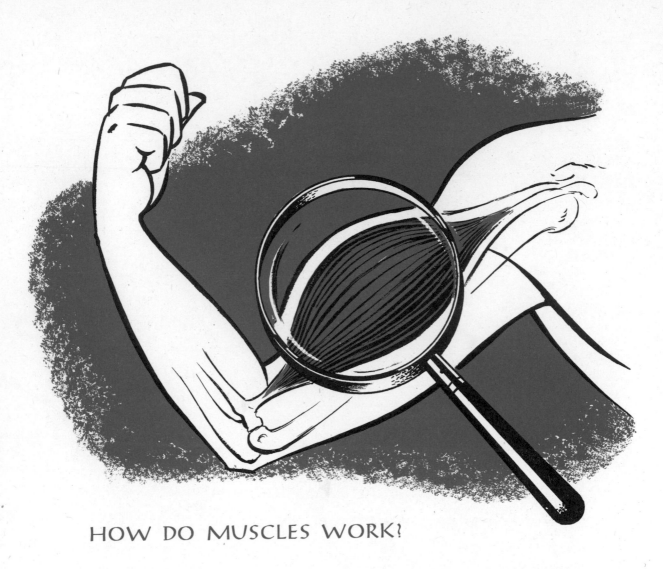

HOW DO MUSCLES WORK?

THIS IS WHAT a piece of muscle looks like when we put it under a magnifying glass. The long, narrow strings are called fibers. Each fiber is made of smaller bits called cells, and each cell has an unbelievably thin wall that separates it from the others. Each is filled with a soft, jelly-like material. And here comes the surprise: The cells are tiny furnaces where a slow fire burns all the time! Of course, the fire doesn't flame or glow. You can't see it. But you can feel it. Your body feels warm because its cells burn fuel.

The fuel for an automobile is gasoline, and burning gasoline makes a car run. Burning coal drives a locomotive. Food burning in the muscle cells gives us muscle power. Scientists have discovered this much. But they still don't know exactly how the wonderful cell furnaces do their part of the work of changing food into muscle power.

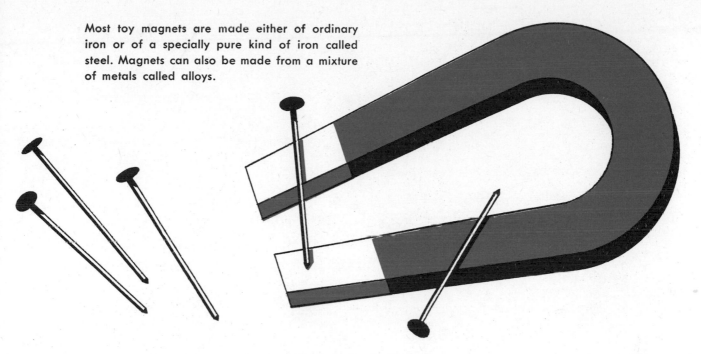

Most toy magnets are made either of ordinary iron or of a specially pure kind of iron called steel. Magnets can also be made from a mixture of metals called alloys.

HOW DOES A MAGNET WORK?

IF YOU EXPERIMENT with a magnet, you will find that it picks up some things but not others. It picks up nails but not gold rings. It picks up needles but not silver spoons. Your magnet is made of a metal called iron, and it will only pick up other things that have a lot of iron in them.

To see how your magnet works, you have to imagine some things first. Imagine that you could cut it in half. Scientists have done so, and they find that they get two separate magnets. Cut one of the halves in two and you get two more magnets. Now imagine you could go on dividing a piece of your iron magnet until you get the smallest possible bit of the metal. This smallest bit is a molecule. Even this molecule is a magnet, too! Every iron molecule is a tiny magnet. It pulls other iron molecules toward itself.

If *all* iron molecules are magnets, then why isn't a nail a magnet? Why can't you pick up a pin with a nail? Scientists think that this is the answer: All the molecules in a nail are mixed up together helter-skelter. Each one pulls on others in a helter-skelter way. But in a magnet the molecules are lined up in an orderly way. They can all make their pull in an orderly way. Their combined pull is so strong that they can draw other separate pieces of iron toward them and pick them up.

IS THE WORLD GETTING WARMER?

PERHAPS you've heard somebody's grandmother say, "Winters aren't as cold as they used to be when I was a girl." Scientists are beginning to think Grandma is right, if she lives in the northeastern part of the United States. That part of the world is warmer than it was fifty years ago. But along the Pacific coast the weather seems to have grown a little colder. Alaska is warming up, and glaciers are melting in other parts of the world. Why? Scientists have made many guesses, but they admit they don't really know. At any rate, if all the ice in the world melted, the oceans would rise at least 200 feet.

WHAT IS ELECTRICITY?

WE KNOW HOW to make electric current in power plants, and we know how to put it to work. But nobody knows exactly what electricity is.

Scientists have figured out that electric current comes from tiny, tiny particles of electricity called electrons. Everything has electrons in it — even you. But the electrons in you don't make an electric current. We get current when machinery in a power plant makes electrons move along a wire. Streams of moving electrons light our houses and heat our toasters and run all of our electrical machines.

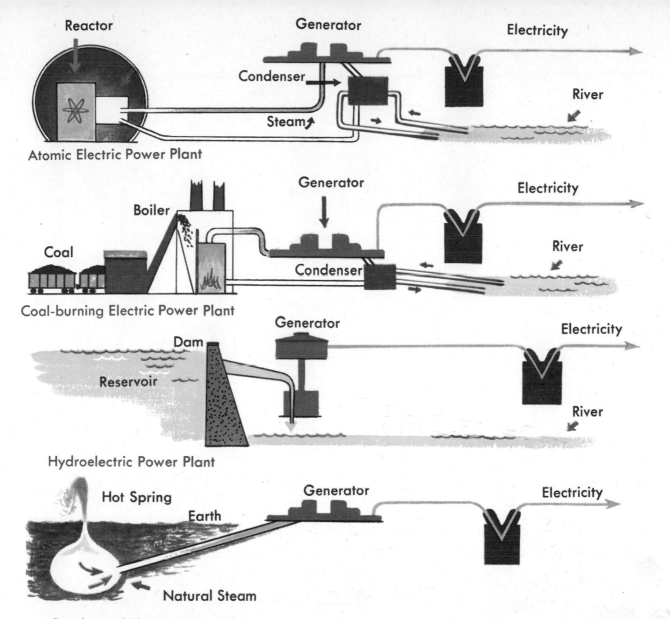

Atomic Electric Power Plant

Coal-burning Electric Power Plant

Hydroelectric Power Plant

Geothermal Electric Power Plant

Here are four power plants. They differ from each other in some ways. But they are alike in another: Each has a generator where electric current is made. Electric current is a stream of electrons moving through a wire. What is needed to make this stream flow? A magnet, for one thing. If you turn a magnet round and round, close to a wire, the electrons in the wire will move. The electrons will also stream along if you whirl a loop of wire close to a magnet. In both cases there is a magnet *plus* whirling motion. And that's what you find in the generator of a power plant.

What makes the generator machinery whirl? Something has to give it a push. Falling water can push wheels round and round. Steam can also push. At the atomic power plant, atomic fuel in the reactor boils the water which becomes steam. At the coal-burning plant, a coal fire heats the water. Both of these plants use the same water over and over. When the steam has given its push in the generator, it goes through a pipe to the condenser. Here it is cooled so that it turns back into water and can flow to the boiler where it again turns to steam. River water, flowing through the condenser in a separate set of pipes, does the cooling.

At the geothermal plant, steam comes from deep inside the earth. It was made there when water trickled down onto very hot rocks.

The hydroelectric plant is run by the force of falling water alone. The water collects behind the dam. Then it rushes down, and its great pushing power makes the generator machinery whirl.

HOW DID ANYBODY EVER FIGURE OUT ALL THE ANSWERS IN THIS BOOK?

No ONE PERSON figured out the answers to all these questions. It took millions of people thousands of years to discover the facts and put them together. But *you* can learn these facts in a day or two. You can do so because part of your body specializes in learning — your *brain*.

Dogs, cats, monkeys — all animals have brains, but yours is a great deal more efficient than any other. Your brain can begin with simple questions. For instance: How does snow smell? Is it good to eat? Does it hurt? After you get the answers, your brain is still not satisfied. It goes right on asking. What makes snow? Where did it *really* come from in the first place?

Questions go on and on. They are always fascinating and they never end. No matter how much men discover, new questions keep turning up. But luckily you don't have to waste time figuring everything out for yourself. You can start with the best answers that brains of men have given so far.

Your brain can store up information and rearrange it and put it together in new combinations. You can invent things entirely inside your head. Then your brain can go on and test an invention to see whether or not it is any good.

How does a brain do all these things? Scientists don't really know. They have made experiments with rats, and they have discovered something interesting about chemicals in the animals' brains. They tested rats that had learned to find the way along a complicated path called a maze. They also tested rats that had not learned to go through the maze. More of a certain chemical appeared in the brains of the rats who had learned the trick!

Was the chemical caused by the learning? Or did the chemical have to be in the brain before learning could begin? Does the same chemical behave in the same way in people's brains? And can scientists find out whether it does? If this chemical helps brains to learn, can you learn faster if you swallow pills made of it? Nobody knows for sure.

Maybe you, by using your brain, will be the one to find out. At any rate you, or someone else, can have a wonderful time trying.

After that mystery has been solved, still others will need to be unraveled. Here are some of them:

What causes the radio signals that come from the vicinity of the planet Venus? These have recently been discovered, but astronomers don't know how the signals are broadcast.

What is sleep and why do we dream? Doctors don't agree on their answers. Experiments have proved that when people dream there is electrical activity in the brain. But it is not clear what this activity means.

Why do living things grow old? We know what happens when people and animals get old — but we don't know the reasons for the changes in their bodies.

What is gravity? Amazing as it may seem, we don't know the answer to this most important question. We know what gravity does and how to measure it. We know that it is different in different places. Its real nature is a mystery.

Where and when did human beings first appear on earth? What were their ancestors like? Perhaps the answer lies buried in a cave somewhere. Perhaps *you* will be the one to find it!

INDEX

Numerals in italics refer to pictures.
Entries printed in capital letters refer to question-titles.

How Do They Get Wild Animals for the Circus and the Zoo?

How Can a Fly Walk on the Ceiling?

What Happens Inside a Cat When It Purrs?

Are Sharks Dangerous?

Where Did the Moon Come From?

How Can Ducks Swim Without Having Lessons?

What Happens to Robins in Winter?

What Makes a Firefly's Light?

What Is Atomic Energy?

How Does a Snake Move?

Do Animals Talk to Each Other?

Why Do Beavers Build Dams?